The Afro-American Novel
1965-1975

The Afro-American Novel
1965-1975

A Descriptive Bibliography of Primary and Secondary Material

by

Helen Ruth Houston

The Whitston Publishing Company
Troy, New York
1977

DEDICATION

In Memory of My Mother

Ruth Louise Hardiman Houston

CONTENTS

Contents

ACKNOWLEDGMENTS

I wish to express my appreciation to Dr. William M. Beasley and the late Dr. Richard C. Peck; to Dr. William J. Connelly, Dr. Wallace R. Maples, Dr. William T. Windham and Dr. Larry V. Lowe for their constant encouragement and assistance. Sincere appreciation is expressed to Dr. Tyree Jones Miller who was consistent and unflinching in her assistance and encouragement. I wish also to acknowledge the aid of Dr. Alberta Barrett; Mrs. Sue P. Chandler, assistant librarian, Special Collection, Fish University; Mrs. Frances Hunter, reference librarian, Middle Tennessee State University; and Dr. Charles Wolfe. My thanks also go to Douglas Barbour of the University of Alberta, Dr. Thomas D. Clareson of College of Wooster and several fanzine editors: Bruce Gillespie, Peter Nicholls, Andrew Porter and Jeffrey Smith. A special debt of gratitude is due Mrs. C. C. Banning, my friend and high school librarian who encouraged my interest in Black literature.

Most of all, I thank my family who performed all of my household duties so that I could spend hours researching materials.

INTRODUCTION

Afro-American literature began more than two centuries ago. It began when people like Lucy Terry, Phillis Wheatley and David Walker felt the need to create and to give the world a description of Negro life in America. Since that time, there has been a continual stream of Black literary works. Yet, our American schools have neglected to include literature by and about Afro-Americans in their English curricula.

Recently, attempts have been made to rectify this neglect. At the local level, a number of institutions recognized that the inclusion of the Black experience as an integral part of the curriculum is necessary to reduce the human relations gap between whites and Blacks.[1] These institutions established numerous Afro-American literature courses to give evidence that the Black man has lived, breathed, fought, labored and created.[2] Other institutions found it more viable, because of a shortage of funds, faculty, and time to "revise curricula to include and emphasize the contributions of Blacks."[3]

At the national level, The National Council of Teachers of English adopted a policy of affirmative action which recommended that ethnic literature be included in all English curricula. As a result of this action, a portion of the larger society now is aware that it is mandatory that the contributions of Afro-Americans be given particular attention since "Racial harmony cannot be attained without a nationwide acceptance and appreciation for cultural differences."[4]

As institutions began attempts to rectify the neglect, they discovered that they lacked information and personnel to implement the curricular changes. Teachers and curriculum writers "who sincerely wish[ed] to incorporate...[Afro-American] literature into their lessons...[were] inadequately prepared to implement the program."[5] Many of these teachers, both Black and white, were Anglo-Saxon oriented. They were unaware of the validity and the educational value of the Black culture, except in a context of debasement and racial denigration. They were not trained to cope with the theory of Black literature. Donald Henderson points out this inadequacy when he states:

> the larger society...fails to acknowledge the existence of black
> people, and subsequently trains teachers and constructs cur-
> ricula and materials for a presumably monolithic white middle-
> class society.[6]

Furthermore, educators were often unaware of what Afro-American literature exists and had "the unfortunate notion that Black writers cannot produce 'literary art'."[7]

Thus, it is imperative that information be made available to these teachers to aid them in effective implementation of Afro-American literature programs. A review of literature revealed a number of bibliographies for teachers and students seeking guides to Afro-American history and culture. There are bibliographies which cover a number of subjects, one of which is literature. Such works are exemplified by *The Negro in the United States: A Research Guide* by Erwin K. Welsch (1965), *A Bibliography of the Negro in Africa and America,* edited by Monroe N. Work (1928) and reprinted in 1966, and *A Working Bibliography on the Negro in the United States* (1968) which was reprinted in 1970 in a modified form as *The Negro in the United States: A Selected Bibliography.* There are specialized bibliographies which pertain only to literature or more specifically the novel. These offer only a listing of works; some offer brief annotations. In this category are *An Annotated Bibliography of Biographies and Autobiographies of Negroes, 1839-1961* by Juanita B. Fuller, "The American Negro and American Literature: A Checklist of Significant Commentaries" in *Bulletin of Bibliography* (September-December 1946) by John S. Lash, "American Negro Literature: A Bibliographical Guide" in *Bulletin of Bibliography* (May-August 1955) by S. H. Kessler, *Bibliographic Survey: The Negro in*

Introduction

Print (contrary to its title, other minority groups are represented), *A Century of Fiction by American Negroes 1853-1952: A Descriptive Bibliography* by Maxwell Whiteman and *Black American Fiction Since 1952: A Preliminary Checklist* by Frank Deodene and William P. French. A more recent listing excluding annotations is "Afro-American Fiction: A Checklist 1853-1970" by Robert Corrigan in *Midcontinent American Studies Journal* (Fall 1970). These are general lists. However, there are bibliographies available in terms of age groups, for instance: *Negro Literature for High School Students* by Barbara Dodd, *We Build Together* by Charlemae Rollins and *The Black Experience in Children's Books* by Augusta Baker. Robert E. McDowell and George Fortenberry have published "A Checklist of Books and Essays about American Negro Novelists" in *Studies in the American Novel* (Summer 1971). This checklist is helpful but is inadequate as an aid for teachers and students interested in serious literary study because it is not comprehensive.

The most useful bibliographic tools for literary scholars seeking a guide to Afro-American literature are those which combine primary and secondary sources. *Blacks in America: Bibliographical Essays* by James M. McPherson, Laurence B. Holland, James Banner, Jr., Nancy J. Weiss and Michael D. Bell includes "100 topics, from Africa to slave trade to life styles in the urban ghettos of 1970"; its entries are annotated. *From the Dark Tower: Afro-American Writers 1900 to 1960* by Arthur P. Davis is a critical and historical study of Afro-American literature; it also contains a selected bibliography of general works and primary and secondary material for the major writers of the period from 1900 to 1960. *Black American Writers Past and Present: A Biographical and Bibliographical Dictionary* by Theressa Gunnels Rush, Carol Fairbanks Myers and Esther Spring Arata lists sources, and in some instances, biographical data and/or quotations from the authors. *Afro-American Writers* by Darwin T. Turner is a comprehensive and scholarly listing; it is cross referenced and divided into five major sections: Aids to Research, Backgrounds, Literary History and Criticism, Afro-American Writers and Selected Criticism of Africans and Afro-Americans as Characters.

Introduction

These bibliographies present Afro-American literature mostly from a sociological approach rather than a literary approach. Only one of these works includes the most recent novelists and criticisms of them. None of these includes annotations of both works and criticism. That educators might approach Afro-American literature from the literary approach, a tool which identifies authors, their works and criticism is necessary. Thus, it is the purpose of this descriptive bibliography to familiarize teachers and students with novels and criticism of Afro-American novelists who have written since 1964. The bibliography is a compilation of works by those Black authors of "Afro-American ancestry who have spent most of their lives in the United States."[8] The authors chosen for inclusion in this work were mentioned in any two of the following Black periodicals: *Black World, CLA Journal, Freedomways, Phylon.* For each author, there is a biographical statement, a descriptive listing of his works since 1964 and a listing of criticism about the author and his works. In some instances, there are also included items by the author which might add to an understanding of his works and philosophy.

Introduction

NOTES

[1]Jean A. Alexander, "Black literature for the 'Culturally Deprived' Curriculum: Who Are the Losers?" *Negro American Literature Forum,* 4 (Fall 1970), p. 97.

[2]Richard A. Long, "The Black Studies Boondoggle," *Liberator,* 10 (September 1970), p. 7.

[3]Inez Smith Reid, ed., *The Black Prism: Perspectives on the Black Experience* (Brooklyn, New York: Faculty Press, 1969), p. 186.

[4]Alexander, p. 96.

[5]Alexander, pp. 99-100.

[6]Donald M. Henderson, "Black Student Protest in White Universities," in *Black America,* ed. John F. Szwed (New York: Basic Books, Inc., 1970), p. 259.

[7]Roger Whitlow, *Black American Literature: A Critical History* (Chicago: Nelson Hall, 1973), p. xiv.

[8]Nick Aaron Ford, "Black Literature and the Problem of Evaluation," *College English,* 32 (February 1971), p. 536.

BIBLIOGRAPHY

The following bibliography is a list of primary and secondary materials for the study of individual Afro-American novelists who have written novels since 1964. The list is divided into four categories: (A) biography, (B) novels by the authors, (C) critical books and articles by and about the author and (D) reviews of the novels printed since 1964. The biographical statement includes in most instances place and date of birth, educational career, awards and honors and work experience. The novels are listed in chronological order. For each entry, a story line is given and in some instances, a comment on technique is included. The annotations of the critical material contain a summary statement, a quote, a listing of the contents, or a combination of these. The annotations of the reviews generally contain a brief quote to indicate the tenor of the review; however, in some instances, there is a summary of the content to indicate the tenor. The novels are again listed in chronological order.

JAMES A. BALDWIN (1924–)

A. James A. Baldwin was born in New York City on August 2, 1924. He is a graduate of DeWitt Clinton High School. He has been awarded a Eugene F. Saxton Fellowship, a Rosenwald Fellowship, a Guggenheim Fellowship, and the National Conference of Christian and Jews Award.

B. Baldwin, James. *Tell Me How Long the Train's Been Gone.* New York: Dial, 1968.

This is the story of Leo Proudhammer, a thirty-nine year old successful actor. He is in the hospital recuperating from a heart attack and recalling his childhood in Harlem, his rise to success and his lovers: white Barbara and Black Christopher.

—. *If Beale Street Could Talk.* New York: Dial, 1974.

The love story of pregnant, nineteen-year-old Tish Rivers and twenty-two-year-old Fronny Hunt, a sculptor, is told. They pledge to marry each other, but before they can marry, he is falsely accused of raping a Puerto Rican woman, arrested and booked. Both the Rivers and the Hunt family set out to find evidence that will free Fronny.

C. Adam, George R. "Black Militant Drama." *American Imago,* 28 (Summer 1971), 107-128.

Blues for Mr. Charlie "is at once a threat to the white society, a statement of Black woe, and a lament for what is dead." This play with its "intelligent, sexually potent angry" protagonist teaches a

8

therapeutic lesson: we must utilize these aggressive energies to create a "new life-style" and to eliminate "all artificial barriers to self-fulfillment."

Alexander, Charlotte. "The 'Stink' of Reality: Mothers and Whores in James Baldwin's Fiction." *Literature and Psychology,* 18 (1968), 9-26.

In Baldwin's fiction, "to remain *clean* is to keep distance, possibly to cling to innocence; to *stink*,...is to become involved...to risk the loss of purity or control." His male characters seldom can confront the stink of reality. He envisions a state when "women who are neither 'mothers' nor 'whores' " would *co-exist* with men, and in this state "reality would no longer stink."

Aptheker, Herbert. "Afro-American Superiority: A Neglected Theme in Literature." *Phylon,* 31 (Winter 1970), 335-343.

James Baldwin is one of the many Black writers who projects the idea of the superiority of Blacks in terms of "ethical and moral superiority...standards of beauty, aesthetic sense and modes and values of life." This is not racism because it is not based on biological or genetic differences.

Auchincloss, Eve and Nancy Lynch. "Disturber of the Peace: James Baldwin." *The Black American Writer, Volume I: Fiction.* Edited by C. W. E. Bigsby. Baltimore, Maryland: Penguin Books Inc., 1971, pp. 199-215.

An interview in which Baldwin discusses liberals, white people, Puritanism, sex, desegregation, hatred, identity and its acceptance.

"Baldwin, James A." *Black American Writers Past and Present: A Biographical and Bibliographical Dictionary.* Theressa Gunnels Rush, Carol Fairbanks Myers and Esther Spring Arata. Metuchen, New Jersey: The Scarecrow Press, Inc., 1975. I, 44-48.

Baldwin's known published works and a selection of Baldwin

criticism are listed.

"Baldwin, James (Arthur)." *Contemporary Authors.* First Revision. Edited by James Ethridge and Barbara Kopala. Detroit, Michigan: Gale Research Company, 1967. I-IV, 44-45.

Biographical data: personal, career, writings, sidelights and biographical/critical sources.

"Baldwin, James." *Contemporary Literary Criticism.* Edited by Carolyn Riley and Barbara Harte. Detroit, Michigan: Gale Research Company, 1974. II, 31-34.

Critical statements on *Another Country, Go Tell It on the Mountain, Notes of a Native Son, Nobody Knows My Name, Tell Me How Long the Train's Been Gone, Blues for Mr. Charlie, The Fire Next Time, No Name in the Street* and Baldwin the writer.

Baldwin, James. *No Name in the Street.* New York: Dial, 1972.

Baldwin reflects over his life and world and attempts to make a statement about what he has seen, felt and known.

—. "Why I Left America, Conversation: Ida Lewis and James Baldwin." *New Black Voices: An Anthology of Contemporary Afro-American Literature.* Edited by Abraham Chapman. New York: Mentor Books, 1972, pp. 409-419.

Baldwin says he left America first because of the mental and spiritual death America has plotted for the Black man. He later returned and had to leave again, for only by leaving could he continue to be himself.

Bennett, Stephen B. and William W. Nichols. "Violence in Afro-American Fiction: An Hypothesis." *Modern Fiction Studies,* 17 (Summer 1971), 221-228.

James Baldwin's *Go Tell It on the Mountain* portrays suicide as a desperate effort to preserve dignity.

Bigsby, C. W. E. "From Protest to Paradox: The Black Writer at Mid Century." *The Fifties: Fiction, Poetry, Drama.* Edited by Warren French. Deland, Florida: Everett/ Edwards, Inc., 1970, pp. 234-240.

Baldwin's central theme is the need to accept reality as a foundation for individual identity and a prerequisite for saving love. He has faith in the saving power of love and is a "sentimentalist in the same sense as Dickens"; he believes in the innate goodness of humanity.

"The Black Scholar Interviews James Baldwin." *Black Scholar,* 5 (December 1973-January 1974), 33-42.

There is a discussion of the Black movements, the universality of the plight of oppressed people, history, racism in France, writing, the poet, Hansberry and the Black family.

Bluefarb, Sam. "James Baldwin's 'Previous Condition' A Problem of Identification." *Negro American Literature Forum,* 3 (Spring 1969), 26-29.

The protagonist in the short story, "Previous Condition," is a Black intellectual; he can be seen as Baldwin himself. He can find his place in neither the Black world nor the white world.

Bone, Robert. "The Novels of James Baldwin." *The Black Novelist.* Edited by Robert Hemenway. Columbus, Ohio: Merrill, 1970, pp. 111-133.

Baldwin is "strongest as an essayist, weakest as a playwright, and successful in the novel form on only one occasion," *Go Tell It on the Mountain.*

This essay also appears in *Tri-Quarterly,* Winter 1965.

Britt, David D. "The Image of the White Man in the Fiction of Langston Hughes, Richard Wright, James Baldwin and Ralph Ellison." Ph.D. dissertation, Emory University,

1968.

Baldwin examines "the more subtle, internalized effects of racism on both Negroes and whites." Thus, the white reader will find it more difficult to recognize himself, for "his fiction does reveal a shortcoming in his grasp of white reality." He shows "a psycho-sexual underpinning for the American treatment of the Negro." "His whites are in spirit much closer to Roger Chillingworth whose commitment to evil is diabolical but bloodless."

Collier, Eugenia. "Thematic Patterns in Baldwin's Essays." *Black World,* 21 (June 1972), 28-34.

The basic assumption of his essays is that life is a wild chaos. His solution to this is an acceptance of self and a facing of "life *absolutely.*" Thus, the answer on a nationwide level is that "we must accept with love, ourselves and each other."

Cosgrove, William. "Strategies of Survival: The Gimmick Motif in Black Literature." *Studies in the Twentieth Century,* Number 15 (Spring 1975), 109-127.

Baldwin stresses the need for finding a survival mechanism in order to live as a Black man in a white world. The gimmicks Baldwin uses in *Go Tell It on the Mountain* are the same ones he has used—intelligence and the church.

Dance, Daryl C. "You Can't Go Home Again: James Baldwin and the South." *CLA Journal,* 18 (September 1974), 80-81.

Baldwin has searched over and over for his roots. He finally found them in the southern part of America but realizes that he cannot go home again. For even though it holds his identity, his manhood, it "threatens to rob him of it and denies him the peace and rest" he expects at home.

Dance, Daryl Cumber. "Wit and Humor in Black American Literature." Ph.D. dissertation, University of Virginia, 1971.

Baldwin shows "little evidence in his fiction of...either laughing or inspiring laughter."

Eckman, Fern Marja. *The Furious Passage of James Baldwin.* New York: Lippincott, 1966.

This is an objective biography of James Baldwin.

Emanuel, James A. "Baldwin, James (Arthur)." *Contemporary Novelists.* Edited by James Vinson. New York: St. Martin's, 1972, pp. 72-75.

Biographical data, list of publications, comments by Baldwin and a discussion of his fiction.

Fabre, Michel. "Fathers and Sons in *Go Tell It on the Mountain,* by James Baldwin." *Etudes Anglaises,* 23 (January-March 1970), 47-61.

Go Tell It on the Mountain is the story of a quest for a father; this theme crops up in all of Baldwin's works more as therapy than literary strategy and at some points may be gimmick. "The novel plays...with a whole constellation of fathers—father unknown and mythical, real and legitimate, putative father, possible father, adulterous husband and father of a bastard—which corresponds to a whole constellation of sons—sons natural, born of adultery, adopted, prodigal, etc."

This essay also appears in *Modern Black Novelists,* edited by M. B. Cooke (Englewood Cliffs, New Jersey: Prentice-Hall, 1971).

Fisher, Russell G. "James Baldwin: A Bibliography, 1947-1962." *Bulletin of Bibliography,* 24 (January-April 1965), 127-130.

Lists works by and about Baldwin.

Foster, David E. " 'Cause my house fell down': The Theme of the Fall in Baldwin's Novels." *Critique,* 3, Number 2, pp. 50-62.

Baldwin explores the theme of man's fall from innocence in his first three novels. His first novel, *Go Tell It on the Mountain*, is a brilliant rendition of the theme because it fuses a traditional Christian motif with a contemporary interpretation. However, the next two books, *Giovanni's Room* and *Another Country*, represent a breakdown in "Baldwin's initial fictional vision." Baldwin attempts to use the same theme with a secular meaning and no redemption, thus making these latter novels poorer.

Gayle, Addison, Jr. *The Way of the New World: The Black Novel in America.* Garden City, New York: Anchor Press/Doubleday, 1975, pp. 213-200.

Baldwin writes in the worst of assimilationists veins, and sees the "black world as atavistic and sensational." When the sensationalism is removed, the "integrationist ethic is revealed."

George, Felicia. "Black Woman, Black Man." *Harvard Journal of Afro-American Affairs,* 2 (1971), 1-17.

Baldwin "took up the theme of the need for finding someone who went before....This person, for Baldwin, is the father. Baldwin does not ignore the female in his search for roots in a father image, but her influence is more subtle."

Gérard, Albert. "The Sons of Ham." *Studies in the Novel,* 3 (Summer 1971), 148-164.

Baldwin explores the psychological results of Black men accepting their color in *Go Tell It on the Mountain* and *Another Country.*

Gibson, Donald B., ed. *Five Black Writers: Essays on Wright, Ellison, Baldwin, Hughes and LeRoi Jones.* New York: New York University Press, 1970, pp. 117-164.

Reprints four essays on Baldwin. "Dark Angel: The Writings of James Baldwin" by Colin MacInnes in which the author sees Baldwin as "colored...[full of] 'dark irony,' " a guardian and an admonisher. "In Defense of James Baldwin" by Normal Podhoretz in which he defends *Another Country*. "Baldwin and the Problem of Being" by George E. Kent in which the author sees Baldwin as not having "evolved the artistic form that will fully release and articulate his obviously complex awareness." "James Baldwin: The Black and the Red-White-and-Blue" by John V. Hagopian in which Baldwin's short story "This Morning, This Evening, So Soon" is discussed.

Gross, Barry. "The 'Uninhabitable Darkness' of Baldwin's *Another Country:* Image and Theme." *Negro American Literature Forum,* 6 (Winter 1972), 113-121.

Baldwin's big and impressively tight novel calls for the realization that "black is not really black and white not really white, that dark is not really dark and the light not really light." It is understood that this realization might not come, but not until man makes the effort to drag "his secrets into the light of the world" can "he escape his private dark dungeon" and without this effort the world would be an unbearable darkness.

Hayashi, Susanna C. "Dark Odyssey: Descent into the Underworld in Black American Fiction." Ph.D. dissertation, Indiana University, 1971.

Baldwin sees "the blackness of the underworld...ultimately as the chaotic and fertile darkness out of which light and order are generated." His characters take a kind of "Dantesque journey...into the underworld of the spirit" and this descent is seen "as a rite of passage."

Hernton, Calvin C. "Blood of the Lamb and a Fiery Baptism." *Amistad 1.* Edited by John A. Williams and Charles F. Harris. New York: Vintage Books, 1970, pp. 183-225.

White America had a love affair going with Baldwin because it did not fear him. However, his play *Blues for Mr. Charlie* caused white America to recoil because it showed an aggressive, masculine Baldwin. Baldwin has become a great writer but "he does not seem to have anything new or different or progressive to say anymore." His motifs keep reappearing.

James A. Baldwin

"James Baldwin—Art or Propaganda?" *Desperate Faith—A Study of Bellow, Salinger, Mailer, Baldwin, and Updike.* Howard M. Harper, Jr. Chapel Hill: University of North Carolina Press, 1967, pp. 137-161.

Baldwin, a popular success and a serious artist, as spokesman for the Black man and artist, expresses slightly different views on the human condition. His stance in the former is that concerted social action could free the Black man; however, the latter sees a great deal of this freedom resulting from each individual's discovery and acceptance of self and involving "this nature with other people, through love."

"James Baldwin." *Dark Symphony: Negro Literature in America.* Edited by James A. Emanuel and Theodore L. Gross. New York: Free Press, 1968, pp. 296-300.

Biographical and critical statement and a brief discussion of *Notes of a Native Son* and "Sonny's Blues."

"James Baldwin: A Fire in the Mind." *The Dark and the Feeling: Black American Writers and Their Work.* Clarence Major. New York: The Third Press, 1974, pp. 73-83.

Chronicles Baldwin's writing career from the beginning to *Tell Me How Long the Train's Been Gone.*

"James Baldwin." *From the Dark Tower: Afro-American Writers 1900 to 1960.* Arthur P. Davis. Washington, D.C.: Howard University Press, 1974, 216-226, 286-289.

Baldwin is a transitional writer; in his early works he was integrationist in leaning, but later "leans heavily toward the black nationalist position." The theme which seems to "run through practically all of James Baldwin's works...[is that] America's great trouble is that it refuses to look objectively at its history and its essential nature."

Kent, George E. *Blackness and the Adventure of Western*

16

Culture. Chicago, Illinois: Third World Press, 1972, pp. 139-151.

Baldwin in his writing "wishes to confront and affect the human consciousness and conscience," but to reach his goal he needs to be as daring in technique as he has been in subject matter.

Kinnamon, Keneth, ed. *James Baldwin, A Collection of Critical Essays.* Twentieth Century Views. Englewood Cliffs, New Jersey: Prentice-Hall, 1974.

The book contains thirteen essays arranged in chronological order: a 1956 Langston Hughes essay to a 1972 Benjamin De Mott essay, an introduction by Kinnamon which addresses Baldwin's importance, a Chronology of Important Dates, Notes on Contributors and a Selected Bibliography. There is a discussion of all of his books except *If Beale Street Could Talk* and the emphasis is on *Go Tell It on the Mountain* and *Another Country*.

Kundt, Kathleen A. "James Baldwin: A Checklist: 1947-1962." *Bulletin of Bibliography*, 24 (January-April 1965), 123-126.

Lists, according to type, works by Baldwin and criticism of Baldwin's work alphabetically.

Lee, Brian. "James Baldwin: Caliban to Prospero." *The Black American Writer. Volume I: Fiction.* Edited by C. W. E. Bigsby. Baltimore, Maryland: Penguin Books, Inc., 1971, pp. 168-179.

Baldwin's first three novels show him arriving at the conclusion that there is "no other country." His fourth novel, *Tell Me How Long the Train's Been Gone,* marks his beginning to tell the truth "in the only language" he has and no longer trying to invent a language.

Lee, Robert A. "James Baldwin and Matthew Arnold: Thoughts on 'Relevance.'" *CLA Journal,* 14 (March 1971), 324-330.

The demands made upon Baldwin are representative of those made upon the Black writer today. He is "expected to be contemporary and appropriate and at the same time unique and original"; he is "caught between sociology and art."

Lewald, H. Ernest, editor. *The Cry of Home: Cultural Nationalism and the Modern Writer.* Knoxville: University of Tennessee Press, 1972, pp. 227-230.

Baldwin's first novel is a major contribution to American literature, an ambitious book. Baldwin interconnects all of the characters, relates them to the rural Southern experience and the consequent urban shock.

Littlejohn, David. *Black on White: A Critical Survey of Writing by American Negroes.* New York: Grossman Publishers, 1966, pp. 72-74, 119-137.

Baldwin's novels, essays and plays are "a symptom of [American] tension [rather] than an examination of it."

Macebuh, Stanley. *James Baldwin: A Critical Study.* New York: Third Press, 1973.

Discusses virtually all Baldwin has written with an emphasis on the novels. His theory is that Baldwin goes from personal preoccupation in the early works to public commitment in the latter. He says the "moral authority and intense passion" of the later work attests to Baldwin's significance as a thinker and writer.

McWhirter, William A. "After Years of Futility Baldwin Explodes Again." *Life,* 30 July 1971, p. 63.

Baldwin was "in calculation" after the death of Martin Luther King, but he has exploded into creativity again.

May, John R. "Images of Apocalypse in the Black Novel." *Renascence,* 23 (Autumn 1970), 31-45.

Baldwin's *Go Tell It on the Mountain* teems with apocalyptic imagery as he "shows the agony and ecstasy of...[the Black man's] simplistic faith—a refuge from white oppression and thus an obstacle to progress."

—. *Toward a New Earth: Apocalypse in the American Novel.* Notre Dame: University of Notre Dame Press, 1972, pp. 145-171.

In *Go Tell It on the Mountain,* a novel which is highly autobiographical and shows Christianity oppressive, Baldwin utilizes Christian images "for purposes of irony." He tries to give a realistic portrayal of the ordinary lives of American Negroes.

Meserve, Walter. "James Baldwin's 'Agony Way.' " *Black American Writer. Volume II: Poetry and Drama.* Edited by C. W. E. Bigsby. Baltimore, Maryland: Penguin Books, Inc., 1971, pp. 171-186.

Baldwin believes the answer to all human problems is love through suffering and this is the theme throughout most of his work. He best illustrates this way of life which he calls the " 'agony way' " by "travelling the same road he adovcates for all others."

Möller, Karin. "James Baldwin's Theme of 'Identity' and His 'Fall' Metaphor." *Essays in Literature,* 2 (March 1974), 34-48.

The phases of the struggle for identity in Baldwin's works are represented in a number of varying contexts—race, art, sexuality, nationality and humanity. This crisis of identity occurs, and it is through the "Fall" metaphor that Baldwin's characters come to terms with human condition.

"The Negro Church: James Baldwin and the Christian Vision." *Native Sons: A Critical Study of Twentieth Century Negro Authors.* Edited by Edward Margolies. Philadelphia: Lippincott, 1968, pp. 102-126.

Baldwin's religious training and early experience in the church influenced his work so that they were a "Christian-Freudian" interpretation of racism.

"Novelist Baldwin Says 'America Is Everywhere.' " *Jet,* 7 January 1971, p. 30.

> Baldwin expresses the universality of America and its problems. The biggest problem is deception, and a change is needed for both Blacks and America.

Reid, Kenneth Russell. "James Baldwin's Fiction: Literary Artistry in Special Pleading." Ph.D. dissertation, Kansas State University, 1972.

> Baldwin, "a minor but nevertheless distinguished" novelist who has never reached the success of his first novel, is seen as speaking not only for himself but also the Black man in his writing. His novels, short stories and plays are explored. *Go Tell It on the Mountain* is his "best because of its thematic richness and structural simplicity." *Giovanni's Room* is "a less-than-successful novel, but...important...[for the] focus of attention, narrative style,...structure." *Another Country* is "overambitious." *Tell Me How Long the Train's Been Gone* represents "no advance to a new level of competence."

Reilly, John M. " 'Sonny's Blues': James Baldwin's Image of Black Community." *Negro American Literature Forum,* 4 (July 1970), 56-60.

> Baldwin presents his leading theme—the discovery of identity—successfully in "Sonny's Blues." Through the use of Blues and its communal nature, Baldwin shows "that artful expression of personal yet typical experience is one way to freedom.

Schraufnagel, Noel. *From Apology to Protest: The Black American Novel.* Deland, Florida: Everett/Edwards, Inc., 1973, pp. 151-153, 185-187.

> Baldwin in *Another Country* joins the realm of the protest novelist and in *Tell Me How Long the Train's Been Gone,* "he joins the rank of militant protest writers."

Shinn, Thelma Wardrop. "A Study of Women Characters in Contemporary American Fiction 1940-1970." Ph.D. dissertation, Purdue University, 1972.

Baldwin's women are "threats to his men" because they are "the only ones strong enough to exist in the world of contemporary American corruption and still...maintain some values." His "women...refuse to compromise when it comes to commitment and love." Generally he sees women as "admirable, unhappy, but struggling human beings" not to be blamed.

Singh, Raman K. "The Black Novel and Its Tradition." *Colorado Quarterly,* 20 (Summer 1971), 23-29.

James Baldwin in *Go Tell It on the Mountain* portrays the Identity-Quest as a discovery of identity rather than the loss of identity.

Standley, Fred L. "James Baldwin: The Artist as Incorrigible Disturber of the Peace." *Southern Humanities Review,* 4 (Winter 1970), 18-30.

Baldwin shows in his novels what he believes "protest" to mean and embodies both sociology and aesthetics.

—. "James Baldwin: A Checklist, 1963-1967." *Bulletin of Bibliography,* 25 (May-August 1968), 135-137, 160.

Lists works by Baldwin, and books, articles and reviews about Baldwin and his work.

Starke, Catherine Juanita. *Black Portraiture in American Fiction; Stock Characters, Archetypes and Individuals.* New York: Basic Books, Inc., 1971, pp. 204-207, 222-225.

Baldwin utilizes the youthful male in search of self in *Go Tell It on the Mountain* and the token Black in *Tell Me How Long the Train's Been Gone* as character types.

Thelwell, Mike. " 'Another Country': Baldwin's New York

Novel." *The Black American Writer. Volume I: Fiction.* Edited by C. W. E. Bigsby. Baltimore, Maryland: Penguin Books, Inc., 1971, pp. 181-198.

The "New York establishment" exhibited a "critical virulence" in its appraisal of *Another Country* because "America's dominant culture group was ill-prepared to cope with a Negro analysis of the culture.

Walton, Martha R. Ballard. "Major Concerns of the Black Novel in America in Relation to the American Mainstream." Ph.D. dissertation, University of Denver, 1973.

Baldwin's novels are ones of protest, but even more he merges with "the American mainstream because of...[his] insights into the human condition."

Whitlow, Roger. *Black American Literature: A Critical History.* Chicago: Nelson Hall, 1973, pp. 127-130.

Biographical data and a brief statement about his work are given.

Williams, Sherley Anne. *Give Birth to Brightness/A Thematic Study of Black Literature.* New York: Dial, 1972, pp. 23, 25-27, 29, 145-166, 223, 225-227.

Baldwin's recurring theme is that "heritage and culture...[are] a sustaining force in the lives of Black people." He utilizes the Black experience to show the hero from a Black point of view. Most of his characters are isolated. He equates white women with death. He sees the secret to "Black survival [as] ...Black love."

D. *Tell Me How Long the Train's Been Gone*

Gilman, Richard. "News from the Novel." *The New Republic,* 17 August 1968, pp. 27-36.

The novel comments on existing and established values rather than making a prophecy of an impersonal and *patient* kind, which fiction does when it is art.

Howe, Irving. "James Baldwin: At Ease in Apocalypse." *Harper's Magazine*, 237 (September 1968), 92-100.

This is "a remarkably bad novel, signaling the collapse of a writer of some distinction." This results from the separation of feeling and voice caused by the number of different roles Baldwin is asked to play.

Llorens, David. Review of *Tell Me How Long the Train's Been Gone* by James Baldwin. *Negro Digest*, 17 (August 1968), 51-52, 85-86.

This is a novel of symbolism and imagery about a Black man's struggle to overcome the definition of himself handed down by whites and the struggle to accept that self he finds and his discovery about the human condition.

Long, Robert Emmet. "From Elegant to Hip." *The Nation*, 10 June 1968, pp. 769-770.

This novel has as its theme failure and the redemptive power of love.

"Milk Run." *Time*, 7 June 1968, p. 104.

The book is redundant in scope; it "rambles like a milk train over the same run that Baldwin covered in *Another Country*, creaks over the same hard ground, sounds the same blast."

Thompson, John. "Baldwin: The Prophet as Artist." *Commentary*, 45 (June 1968), 67-69.

This is "a masterpiece by one of the best living writers in America" which will offer little comfort and cheer and may "move you to tears."

If Beale Street Could Talk

Aldridge, John W. "The Fire Next Time?" *Saturday Review/World,* 15 June 1974, pp. 20, 24-25.

This is a novel which is "junk" and further underscores the deteriorating of a Black writer who gained his fame on anger and rage, into the vice of sentimentality.

Edwards, Thomas R. "Can You Go Home Again?" *New York Review of Books,* 13 June 1974, pp. 38-39.

This book cannot be read as accurate social drama; it fails to make the reader believe the horror that really exists.

Flamer, Merrianne. "Another Good Book by Man of Letters." *Freedomways,* 14 (1974), 356-359.

"This is perhaps not Baldwin's most controversial or 'important' book, but...in its decency and compassion, we return with him to those simple and enduring values and realities of Black life."

McCluskey, John. Review of *If Beale Street Could Talk* by James Baldwin. *Black World,* 24 (December 1974), 51-52, 88-90.

By using the blues framework (the title comes from a W. C. Handy line), Baldwin is able to synthesize some of his concerns and construct his most convincing novel. The sense of family and hope survive the ordeals for "the Riverses are...loving, demanding, enduring, not maudlin angels or dreary victims of superfolk."

Oates, Joyce Carol. Review of *If Beale Street Could Talk* by James Baldwin. *The New York Times Book Review,* 19 May 1974, pp. 1-2.

This is "a quite moving and very traditional celebration of love."

Review of *If Beale Street Could Talk* by James Baldwin. *Black Books Bulletin,* 3 (Fall 1975), 42-43.

"Baldwin is good in this book because the story is entirely credible; he has dipped his pen in the survival pulses of Black America."

Webster, Ivan. Review of *If Beale Street Could Talk* by James Baldwin. *New Republic,* 15 June 1974, pp. 25-26.

This is a major work by Baldwin, but an unlikely one for him in its hope, affirmation and mordantly comic tone. The bluesman title is a jest.

BARRY BECKHAM (1944—)

A. Barry Beckham was born in Philadelphia, Pennsylvania, on March 19, 1944. He attended Brown University, New York University School of Continuing Education, and Columbia University Law School. He has worked in public relations and as a lecturer. One of his novels has been sold to a company for production as a film.

B. Beckham, Barry. *My Main Mother.* New York: Walker and Company, 1971.

Mithell Mibbs has murdered his mother. In a series of flashbacks, his relationship with his uncle and his mother is explored. After the death of his uncle, his friend and idol, he has a disagreement with his mother and kills her.

—. *Runner Mack.* New York: Morrow, 1972.

The novel explores two characters, Henry Adams and Runnington Mack. Henry Adams leaves the South for the North hoping to play baseball with the magic N.Y. Stars but ends up taking a job in a factory to support Beatrice, his wife. Adams is actually searching for meaning and identity. He gains this, partially, when he meets Runnington Mack, a revolutionary.

C. "Beckham, Barry." *Black American Writers Past and Present: A Biographical and Bibliographical Dictionary.* Theressa Gunnels Rush, Carol Fairbanks Myers and Esther Spring Arata. Metuchen, New Jersey: The Scarecrow Press, Inc., 1975. I, 66-67.

Biographical data, published works and reviews of his works are listed.

"Beckham, Barry." *Contemporary Authors.* Edited by Clare D. Kinsman and Mary Ann Tennenhouse. Detroit, Michigan: Gale Research Company, 1972. XXIX-XXXII, 48-49.

Biographical data: personal, career, writings, sidelights, avocational interests and biographical/critical sources.

Land, Irene Stokvis, editor. "First Novelists." *Library Journal,* 94 (October 1, 1969), 3473.

Beckham gives some biographical data and discusses his concerns in *My Main Mother,* images and ideas for his next novel and the characteristics of the best fiction.

Pinsker, Sanford. "About *Runner Mack:* An Interview with Barry Beckham." *Black Images,* 3 (Autumn 1974), 35-41.

Discusses the main character's name, Henry Adams, in terms of its symbolical possibilities and relation to other works, such as *The Education of Henry Adams* and *Invisible Man.* He says that in his work he is aiming for "an unnatural, gothic quality," surrealism.

—. "A Conversation with Barry Beckham." *Studies in Black Literature,* 5 (Winter 1974), 17-20.

26

He discusses a Black aesthetic which means a grounding in a sense of history (an inclusion of African and American form), the response of the Black community to the Black artist, the question of publishing with a Black publisher, Afro-American literature, writing in general and Black films.

D. *My Main Mother*

Coombs, Orde. Review of *My Main Mother* by Barry Beckham. *Negro Digest,* 19 (February 1970), 77-79.

This is "a tragedy that is poignant and sad, and in spite of its horrendous theme of matricide, totally believable."

Rowley, Peter. Review of *My Main Mother* by Barry Beckham. *The New York Times Book Review,* 30 November 1969, pp. 64-65.

This is basically "a psychological study of the ruinous effect on a child who is either ignored or tormented by a parent." It follows the anti-parent novel tradition.

Runner Mack

Walker, Jim. Review of *Runner Mack* by Barry Beckham. *Black Creation,* 4 (Winter 1973), 62-63.

This is a novel which in a satiric manner chronicles Henry Adams' never-ending search for himself.

Watkins, Mel. Review of *Runner Mack* by Barry Beckham. *The New York Times Book Review,* 27 September 1972, pp. 3, 50.

Baseball is the central metaphor in this allegorical novel and "Beckham's satire and burlesque are effective."

HAL BENNETT (1930—)

A. Hal Bennett was born in Buckingham, Virginia, on April 21, 1930. From 1953-1955, he was fiction editor for the *Afro-American* newspaper. He attended college in Mexico City.

B. Bennett, Hal. *A Wilderness of Vines.* Garden City, New York: Doubleday, 1966.

The importance of color and the role it plays in the lives of the Negroes of Burnside, Virginia, a farming community of plantations worked by dark skinned or black Negroes, is the focus of this novel. The story takes place between 1920 and 1939. Exposed here is the imitation of the white code of discrimination by color.

—. *The Black Wine.* Garden City, New York: Doubleday, 1968.

David Hunter, his sister, and his mother live happily in Virginia for a period. However, when he is seven, he hears his mother say she loves his half-white sister better than him. Soon after this, tragedy strikes, and the family moves to Newark, New Jersey. When his mother arrives there, she, takes up with the Jewish landlord. David resents this; finally, he and his mother have a confrontation.

—. *Lord of Dark Places.* New York: Norton, 1970.

Roosevelt, the husband of Madam Eudora who founded The Church of Stephen Martyr, tries to carry on her religion after her

death. However, he is hanged becaue he winked at a white woman.
His son Titus sees this hanging and flees vowing that his son will
not die like Roosevelt. Titus later founds a religion—The Church
of the Naked Disciple—in which the phallus is worshiped. His
son, Joe, is used in the service. Joe later travels alone still using
the phallus as a weapon and an idol.

—. *Wait Until Evening.* Garden City, New York: Doubleday, 1974.

Kevin, a nine-year-old, narrates the story of the Brittain family,
three generations of Black Virginia sharecroppers. The family
splits up—part remain in Virginia and part go to New Jersey.
Kevin goes to New Jersey and later returns to the South. In his
travels, he is pursued by a weird white policeman.

C. "Bennett, Hal." *Living Black American Authors: A Biographical Directory.* Ann Allen Shockley and Sue P.
Chandler. New York: Bowker, 1973, p. 12.

Biographical data: birth, professional experience, publication
and mailing address.

Walcott, Ronald. "The Novels of Hal Bennett: The Writer
as Magician/Priest, Part II." *Black World,* 23 (July 1974),
78-96.

Lord of Dark Places is a satirical and all but scatalogical attack on
the phallic myth. Bennett attempts to counter the myth of the
phallus with the myth of innocence—the controlling myth of his
fiction. The novel "insists that even in madness there is hope."

—. "The Novels of Hal Bennett: The Writer as Satirist, Part
I." *Black World,* 23 (June 1974), 36-48, 89-97.

Bennett's first three novels—*A Wilderness of Vines, The Black
Wine* and *Lord of Dark Places*—are satires. The important thematic
concerns of these satires—"his interest in myth and archetype and
their recurrence in patterns of social behavior bordering on the

surreal"—are "the controlling imagery and metaphor of his fiction."

D. *The Black Wine*

Wright, Charles. "New Jersey Street Scene." *The New York Times Book Review,* 5 May 1968, p. 36.

This is a novel of David Hunter's violent coming of age. The book gives the "feeling that the author was torn between a critical success and a commercial success."

Lord of Dark Places

"Ugly Odyssey." *Times Literary Supplement,* 11 December 1971, p. 1427.

Bennett attacks the phallic myth by "bringing the myth home to roost by offering as his hero the 'nigger stud' personified."

Wait Until Evening

Sharpe, Lynn. Review of *Wait Until Evening* by Hal Bennett. *Encore American and Worldwide News,* 6 January 1975, pp. 25-26.

This is a book of perversity and violence, of "Blacks struggling to live in a world hell-bent on their destruction."

ROBERT BOLES (1944–)

B. Boles, Robert. *Curling.* Boston: Houghton, 1968.

Chelsea Meredith Burlingame's thoughts and memories are recorded over a period of a weekend when he leaves his job as a structural engineer, visits friends, walks the streets of Boston, attends a party and gets into a brawl. He becomes aware of himself as the reader becomes aware of his life story. He is a Negro who has been adopted by a white family.

C. Bellamy, Joe David. "Theme and Structure in Boles' *Curling:* An Interview with the Author." *Black Academy Review,* 1 (Spring 1970), 31-39.

The conversation in the novel moves along on the "edge of understandability or non-understandability" because to Boles this is the way people actually talk. The main character, Chelsea, is uncertain; his uncertainty results from his lack of knowledgable history. Boles says he is not concerned with race in his writing. Other topics discussed are Black writers, Black literature courses, his influences and the status of the novel.

Billingsley, Ronald G. "The Burden of the Hero in Modern Afro-American Fiction." *Black World,* 25 (December 1975), 38-45, 66-73.

Robert Boles' short story "The Engagement Party" points up the difficulty of taking on the "economic and social characteristics of the white middle class without simultaneously acquiring all of their definitions and pathologies."

Schraufnagel, Noel. *From Apology to Protest: The Black American Novel.* Deland, Florida: Everett/Edwards, Inc., 1973, pp. 125, 154-155.

Curling stresses the "absurdity of man's condition in a chaotic universe." Boles' first novel, *The People One Knows,* "emphasizes the prejudice of Americans in a European setting."

D. *Curling*

Dempsey, David. "Between Two Worlds." *The New York Times Book Review,* 3 March 1968, p. 40.

The book never "really comes to grips with its big ideas" but it is an honest novel. This is a sensitive novel; therein lies its problem which "rewards in dozens of small compelling ways."

Giovanni, Nikki. Review of *Curling* by Robert Boles. *Negro Digest,* 17 (August 1968), 86-88.

Curling is a disappointment, for it says "we've just got to adjust to the American situation."

Greenya, John. "A Colorless Sort of Gray." *Saturday Review,* 17 February 1968, p. 38.

The title refers to the Scottish game, to Chelsea's response to life and to Boles' narrative method.

Miller, Thomas. Review of *Curling* by Robert Boles. *Commonweal,* 21 June 1968, pp. 419-420

This is "a novel about miniature events" in which "everything... is...out of style." The idea, Black man worrying about being white, is a good one, but Boles "blew it."

CECIL M. BROWN

B. Brown, Cecil M. *The Life and Loves of Mr. Jiveass Nigger; A Novel.* New York: Farrar, 1970.

The story of George Washington alias Paul Winthrop, Jr., alias Julius Maxwell, alias Anthony Miller, a young Black is told. His sexual adventure in the South, in Harlem and Copenhagen enable him finally to find his identity and to return to America which he both loves and hates.

C. Brown, Cecil. "Bad Writing or Unclewillieandthebadpoet." *Partisan Review,* 39 (Summer 1972), 406-411.

"Young writers (especially black writers)" must create a new style, one that is radical, new in content and form and contains paradox. There is no such thing as "good writing," all " 'good writing' is 'bad.' " Subject matter is not important as long as the media is mixed.

Fenderson, Lewis H. "The New Breed of Black Writers and Their Jaundiced View of Tradition." *CLA Journal,* 15 (September 1971), 18-24.

Cecil Brown in his novel shows "a new relationship between the black man and the artless white female."

Klotman, Phyllis R. "The White Bitch Archetype in Contemporary Black Fiction." *Bulletin of the Midwest Modern Language Association,* 6 (Spring 1973), 96-110.

Ruth Smith, the bitch in Brown's *The Life and Loves of Mr. Jiveass Nigger,* is a fading Oklahoma "cracker," who is "less educated than the black men...[she] want[s] to seduce." She is rejected by Jiveass and this rejection "brings about her destruction."

Schraufnagel, Noel. *From Apology to Protest: The Black American Novel.* Deland, Florida: Everett/Edwards, Inc., 1973, pp. 132-133.

The Life and Loves of Mr. Jiveass Nigger develops the theme that to fulfill the role assigned by whites, the Negro is in danger of losing his individuality.

D. *The Life and Loves of Mr. Jiveass Nigger*

Elder, Lonne, III. Review of *The Life and Loves of Mr. Jiveass Nigger* by Cecil Brown. *Black World,* 19 (June 1970), 51-52.

The merit of the book is not its story line, but what it says about Black life-style and ritual.

ED BULLINS (1935—)

A. Ed Bullins was born in Philadelphia, Pennsylvania, on July 2, 1935. He attended William Penn Business School in Philadelphia, Los Angeles City College, and San Francisco State College. He has won the Vernon Rice Award, a Rockefeller Foundation grant and an American Place Theater grant.

B. Bullins, Ed. *The Reluctant Rapist.* New York: Harper, 1973.

Steve Bronson's initiation into life is explored. The story moves from his youth on the Eastern Shore of Maryland to his teen-age days in Philadelphia and his adult life in Los Angeles. By the end of the novel, the only thing which keeps him vibrant is rape.

C. Anderson, Jervis. "Profiles." *New Yorker,* 16 June 1973, pp. 40-49.

Discusses Bullins' life, his craft, his work in the theater (especially the New Lafayette), his ideas about Black theater, his critics, his plays and briefly mentions *The Reluctant Rapist.*

Ed Bullins

"Bullins, Ed." *Black American Writers Past and Present: A Biographical and Bibliographical Dictionary.* Theressa Gunnels Ruch, Carol Fairbanks Myers and Esther Spring Arata. Metuchen, New Jersey: The Scarecrow Press, Inc., 1975. I, 122-125.

Biographical data: birth, professional experience, memberships, awards, publications, and address.

Dance, Daryl Cumber. "Wit and Humor in Black American Literature." Ph.D. dissertation, University of Virginia, 1971.

Bullins is one of the authors Dance uses to develop her thesis that contemporary Black humor "lacks the positive aspects and optimism that frequently characterize black humor." This, in spite of the fact that "it has its root in early black folklore and...continues trends established by previous black writers."

Evans, Don. "The Theater of Confrontation: Ed Bullins, Up Against the Wall." *Black World,* 23 (April 1974), 14-18.

Bullins is "concerned with those suicidal practices that render the Black man impotent....His concentration is on the community as it is, as he sees it now."

Giles, James R. "Tenderness in Brutality: The Plays of Ed Bullins." *Players,* 48 (October-November 1972), 32-33.

In the Wine Time, In New England Winter and *Goin' a Buffalo* illustrate "the theme of a brutal reality destroying human dreams of tenderness and romance." There is in these plays "a mood of lost innocence, purity, and beauty."

Hay, Samuel A. "What Shape Shapes Shapelessness?: Structural Elements in Ed Bullin's [sic] Plays." *Black World,* 23 (April 1974), 20-26.

"The search for structure [in *The Duplex*] ... must focus not on

35

the development of action, but on the development of the theme, the recurrence of hopes for Self-completeness." This structural style is the same as that found in the works of the Russian playwright Chekhov.

Jackson, Kennell, Jr. "Notes on the Works of Ed Bullins and *The Hungered One.*" *CLA Journal,* 18 (December 1974), 292-299.

The Hungered Ones, a collection of the earliest works of Bullins, reveals the germs of the work which later becomes his realistic works. These works have characters who live on the fringes of American culture, but they seem to thrive on the chaos that surrounds them.

Kroll, Jack. "In Black America." *Newsweek,* 20 March 1972, pp. 98-99.

A discussion of the argument over the production of *The Duplex,* one of the plays from his projected twenty-play cycle.

Marvin X. "Black Theater: An Interview with Ed Bullins." *Negro Digest,* 18 (April 1969), 9-16.

Discussed are Bullins' anthology and some of his plays, the new Black theater and the Lafayette theater, the Black arts movement as a whole and the writer who influenced him.

O'Brien, John. "Interview with Ed Bullins." *Negro American Literature Forum,* 7 (Fall 1973), 108-111, back cover.

He discusses his influences, propaganda and art, a writer's responsibility, publishing, Black literature, theatre, his themes and his fiction.

Smitherman, Geneva. "Everybody Wants to Know Why I Sing the Blues." *Black World,* 23 (April 1974), 4-13.

"Bullins has merged the best of tradition with his own (Black) individual talent." He integrates his revolutionary message by utilizing the blues motif. In this way he says, "we must look where we have been, re-examine the 'brutal' Black experience."

Trotta, Geri. "Not to be Missed: Black Theater." *Harper's Bazaare,* August 1968, pp. 150-153.

Bullins' "plays are black to the core" and illuminate "problems... with a poignancy no social worker's statistics can begin to convey."

Wesley, Richard. "An Interview with Playwright Ed Bullins." *Black Creation,* 4 (Winter 1973), 8-10.

He discusses critics, his works and Black theater: what it is, who should criticize and images on the stage.

D. *The Reluctant Rapist*

Bryant, Jerry H. "The Outskirts of a New City." *The Nation,* 12 November 1973, pp. 501-502, 504.

This "isn't a philosophical novel. It is a novel of the felt texture of living, especially of living black." He has not only a mastery of technique, but also a confidence in himself as a writer and what he observes.

Davis, George. Review of *The Reluctant Rapist* by Ed Bullins. *The New York Times Book Review,* 30 September 1973, p. 24.

This book, which deals with Black life before the Black consciousness, has the same stubborn honesty of his plays.

Hord, Fred. "But We Need More!" *Black Books Bulletin,* 2 (Spring 1974), 10, 12, 14.

This "in the traditional sense of the Western novel...is good." However, more than demonstrate Black people's ability to survive, he needs to provide "directions for terminating" the plight of the street Blacks.

McClain, Ruth Rambo. Review of *The Reluctant Rapist* by Ed Bullins. *Black World*, 24 (December 1974), 93-94.

The novel belies its title; it is about survival. He utilizes both flashback and stream of consciousness style.

GEORGE CAIN (1943—)

A. George Cain was born in New York City, in 1943. He attended public and private schools in the city and entered Iona College. He left college in his junior year to travel and spent some time in California, Mexico, Texas and prisons. He returned to New York City in 1966.

B. Cain, George. *Blueschild Baby.* New York: McGraw-Hill, 1970.

This is the story of a young Black man's return to Harlem and the upper West Side after "doing time" in Texas. His present existence confronts his past in a series of encounters after he returns.

C. Billingsley, Ronald G. "The Burden of the Hero in Modern Afro-American Fiction." *Black World*, 25 (December 1975), 38-45, 66-73.

George Cain in *Blueschild Baby* is fortunate in that he has assistance in his "quest for healthy self-definition and freedom." However, he is isolated by his society and the futile way in which he attempts to cope with it.

D. *Blueschild Baby*

Gayle, Addison, Jr. Review of *Blueschild Baby* by George
Cain. *The New York Times Book Review,* 17 January
1971, pp. 4, 34-35.

The novel "represents a major breakthrough for the black writer...
the most important work of fiction by an Afro-American since
'Native Son.' "

Kent, George E. "Struggle for the Image: Selected Books
by or About Blacks During 1971." *Phylon,* 33 (Winter
1972), 304-323.

It is "interesting both for its subject...its struggle for identity and
more positive relations to the so-called ghetto."

McCluskey, John. Review of *Blueschild Baby* by George
Cain. *Black World,* 20 (September 1971), 93-95.

"Cain has demonstrated the possibilities inherent in a skillful
blend of the tone of the personal essay with the thrust of the
naturalistic novel."

Major, Clarence. Review of *Blueschild Baby* by George
Cain. *Essence,* 2 (August 1971), 26.

The author is "honest and even passionate" and the writing has a
"very promising quality." This review also appears in *The Dark
and Feeling* by Clarence Major.

Meaddough, R. J. "Another Shallow Novel of Ghetto
Life." *Freedomways,* 11 (1971), 207-208.

The book is not bad but shallow, written for a white audience,
more autobiographical than novelistic and has little to do with
real Black people.

ALICE CHILDRESS (1920—)

A. Alice Childress was born in Charleston, South Carolina, in 1920. She attended Radcliffe Institute for Independent Study. She is an actress, writer and lecturer. She was director of the American Negro Theatre in New York for twelve years.

B. Childress, Alice. *A Hero Ain't Nothin' But a Sandwich.* New York: Coward, McCann and Geoghegan, Inc., 1973.

The story of thirteen-year-old Benjie Johnson who begins smoking "pot" and gives it up for heroin. The story is of his addiction and the attempts to rehabilitate him. His story is told in his words and those close to him: his mother, stepfather, grandmother, friend, teachers, the principal and his main connection.

C. "Alice Childress." *American Black Women in the Arts and Social Sciences: A Bibliographic Survey.* Ora Williams. Metuchen, New Jersey: The Scarecrow Press, Inc., 1973, p. 64.

Lists books, plays, short stories and articles by Childress and an article of criticism.

"Childress, Alice." *Black American Writers Past and Present: A Biographical and Bibliographical Dictionary.* Theressa Gunnels Rush, Carol Fairbanks Myers and Esther Spring Arata. Metuchen, New Jersey: The Scarecrow Press, Inc., 1975. I, 149-151.

Biographical data and works by and about her are listed.

"Childress, Alice." *Contemporary Authors.* Edited by Clare D. Kinsman. Detroit, Michigan: Gale Research Company, 1974. XLV-XLVIII, 93.

Biographical data: personal, career, writings, work in progress, sidelights.

"Conversation with Alice Childress and Toni Morrison/The Co-Editors." *Black Creation Annual* (1974-75), pp. 90-92.

Childress discusses criticism and major themes and ideas in today's Black writing.

Dance, Daryl Cumber. "Wit and Humor in Black American Literature." Ph.D. dissertation, University of Virginia, 1971.

One of the writers used to support the author's thesis that today's Black humor lacks the positive and optimistic quality of early Black folklore is Alice Childress.

Mitchell, Loften. "Three Writers and a Dream." *Crisis,* 72 (April 1965), 219-223.

Childress' style and theme as a playwright are discussed. Emphasis is on her play *Wedding Band.*

D. *A Hero Ain't Nothin' But a Sandwich*

Rogers, Norma. "To Destroy Life." *Freedomways,* 14 (1974), 72-75.

Childress "has presented an examination of society on the decline in the United States."

CYRUS COLTER (1910–)

A. Cyrus Colter was born in Noblesville, Indiana, on January 8, 1910. He attended Youngstown University, Ohio State University and Chicago-Kent College of Law. His work experience includes deputy collector of internal revenue, captain in the United States Army and attorney. Awards he has received include the Patron Saints Award of the Society of Midland and the $1000 Iowa School of Letters Awards for short fiction.

B. Colter, Cyrus. *The Rivers of Eros.* Chicago: Swallow, 1972.

> Clothilda Pilgrim has devoted all of her time and energy to rearing her two grandchildren. However, she is haunted by the fact that her only child, Rosie, was by her brother-in-law. She is finally forced to face her past when her granddaughter becomes involved with a man.

—. *The Hippodrome.* Chicago: Swallow, 1973.

> Parker nee Yaeger is a Bible-toting middle-aged Black man who decapitates his wife, walks around with her head under his arm and is finally locked up in a house of ill repute that specializes in kinky sexual floor shows. One of the prostitutes falls in love with him and tries to get him to flee the house and reform.

C. "Colter, Cyrus." *Black American Writers Past and Present: A Biographical and Bibliographical Dictionary.* Theressa Gunnels Rush, Carol Fairbanks Myers and Esther Spring

Arata. Metuchen, New Jersey: The Scarecrow Press, Inc., 1975. I, 167-168.

Biographical data, criticism and his published works are listed.

"Colter, Cyrus." *Living Black American Authors: A Biographical Directory.* Ann Allen Shockley and Sue P. Chandler. New York: Bowker, 1973, pp. 32-33.

Biographical data: birth, education, family, professional experience, memberships, awards, publications and address.

"Cyrus Colter." *Interviews with Black Writers.* Edited by John O'Brien. New York: Liveright, 1973, pp. 17-33.

Colter explores "the existential and deterministic nature of man's existence," man's inability to articulate and the problem of being human not necessarily Black or white. He sees tragedy as an affirmation of life and feels he was influenced by Hobbes, Skinner and Camus. He discusses the stories in *The Beach Umbrella* and his novel *The Rivers of Eros.*

"Cyrus Colter, Northwestern." *People,* 13 October 1975, p. 61.

Colter's present working condition is discussed.

Farnsworth, Robert M. "Conversation with Cyrus Colter." *New Letters,* 39 (Spring 1973), 17-39.

He discusses his reasons for writing and some of his stories.

O'Brien, John. "Forms of Determinism in the Fiction of Cyrus Colter." *Studies in Black Literature,* 4 (Summer 1973), 24-28.

Colter is concerned with philosophical problems, not the Black experience even though his characters are Black. The lives of his characters are determined by the past, sexual fears, guilt, accident and chance. Colter's determinism is made terrifying by the hope lessness of his world and the sense that life itself is without meaning. His characters "are lost and determined in a world that is absurd."

D. *The River of Eros*

Blades, John. Review of *The River of Eros* by Cyrus Colter. *Book World,* 18 June 1972, p. 1.

This is a novel written in the author's language, not the usual novelistic language, which examines in a very capable manner "the interior lives of ordinary, unnoticed people."

Kent, George E. "Outstanding Works in Black Literature During 1972." *Phylon,* 34 (December 1973), 307-329.

This flawed novel illustrates that "dimension of Black life which is self-generating."

The Hippodrome

Turner, Darwin T. Review of *The Hippodrome* by Cyrus Colter. *Black World,* 23 (February 1974), 77-79.

This is a novel which has unbelievable characters, no myths, symbols, or social criticism.

CLARENCE COOPER, JR.

B. Cooper, Clarence L., Jr. *The Farm.* New York: Crown.

The Farm is a federal narcotics prison in the South. This is the story of John, an intelligent and rebellious Negro, and his sojourn there. He attempts to concern himself only with his own problem, but he meets and becomes involved with Sonja of the women's ward.

D. *The Farm*

Morton, Eric. "A Black Hamlet in a White Whale's Belly." *Freedomways,* 7 (1967), 375-377.

Cooper is intent on portraying the Black ghettos of America, minus the "distraction of Pollyanna, pedestrian language and morals."

GEORGE DAVIS

A. George Davis was in the United States Air Force for seven years and was discharged after flying forty-seven missions over Vietnam 1967-1968. He is a former reporter for the Washington *Post* and former deskman for the *New York Times.* He teaches at Bronx Community College. His fiction has appeared in *Black World, Black Review* and *Amistad 1.*

B. Davis, George. *Coming Home.* New York: Random House, 1971.

The story of three United States fighter pilots in Thailand, the women they left at home and their women in Indochina is told. The novel explores the way war affects men's moral attitudes toward violence, love and sex. It is about race—how Childress and Ben (Black) and Stacy (white) react to hostility among themselves and between themselves and the people they are supposed to defend.

C. Land, Irene Stokvis, editor. "First Novelists." *Library Journal,* 96 (October 1, 1971), 3164.

Statement by Davis about his life and writing.

Beauford, Fred. "A Conversation with First Novelist George Davis." *Black Creation,* 3 (Spring 1972), 16-17.

Davis discusses the Vietnam War, his novel and Black writing.

NOLAN DAVIS (1942—)

A. Nolan Davis was born in Kansas City, Missouri, on July 23, 1942. He attended the United States Navy Journalist School and Stanford University. He has been editor, staff writer, producer, scriptwriter and director. He is presently an independent writer and producer.

B. Davis, Nolan. *Six Black Horses.* New York: Putman's, 1971.

This is the tale of Lawrence Xavier Jordan who rises to fame and fortune as the leading Black mortician of Kansas City, Missouri. Southwall Lovingood at the urging of Jordan's mother, Clare, takes Jordan under his wing. Lawrence Jordan, artist at heart, becomes quickly indoctrinated into the "artistic" aspects of the undertaking profession. He meets Sister Fannie Lartarska Fears who owns the "Pink Pagoda" mortuary and runs a fleet of pink cadillac hearses. He also meets the perennial mourner Sister Carrier Samuels who is so impressed with Jordan's work she gives him the ultimate compliment—she promises him her body when she dies.

C. "Davis, Nolan." *Black American Writers Past and Present: A Biographical and Bibliographical Dictionary.* Theressa Gunnels Rush, Carol Fairbanks Myers and Esther Spring Arata. Metuchen, New Jersey: The Scarescrow Press, Inc., 1975. I, 205-206.

Biographical data, a photograph, a list of "all published books," and a statement by Davis.

"Davis, Nolan." *Contemporary Authors.* Edited by Clare D. Kinsman. Detroit, Michigan: Gale Research Company, 1975. XLIX-LII, 142-143.

Biographical data: personal, career, writings, work in progress, sidelights and biographical/critical sources.

Land, Irene Stokvis, editor. "First Novelists." *Library Journal,* 96 (October 1, 1971), 3164-3165.

Nolan Davis talks about his novel Six Black Horses.

D. *Six Black Horses*

Grosvenor, Dorothy. Review of *Six Black Horses* by Nolan Davis. *Essence,* 2 (February 1971), 62.

"Nolan Davis has demonstrated a fine comedic talent that is tinged with irony and a true ring for Black vernacular. He has taken...a grim subject and wittily and knowledgeably written about it."

SAMUEL R. DELANY (1942—)

A. Samuel R. Delany was born April 1, 1942. He grew up in New York City's Harlem. He attended The Dalton Elementary School, the Bronx High School of Science and City College. He wrote his first science fiction novel, *The Jewels of Aptor,* when he was nineteen and his trilogy, *The Fall of the Towers,* at twenty-one. He has traveled in France, Italy, Greece, Turkey and England.

B. Delany, Samuel R. *The Ballad of Beta-2.* New York: Ace Books, 1965.

> Joneny, a student of galactic anthropology, is sent on a quest to find the meaning of the Ballad of Beta-2. This is the only clue that even hints at what happened to spaceship Beta-2's missing crew of galactic colonists.

—. *Babel-17.* New York: Ace Books, 1966.

> There is an interstellar war and the communications weapon is Babel-17. It has the power to disrupt the space-communications system of the Earthpeople Alliance. The only hope is that Rydra Wong, a cosmic poetess who comprehends all tongues, is able to decipher the power of Babel-17.

—. *Empire Star.* New York: Ace Books, Inc., 1966.

> This is the story of Comet Jo, the cat-bodied star wanderer. He meets in his travels: the Lump, a half-alien, half machine; Ni Ty Lee, the suicidal poet of the stars; the multiplex conscious called Jewel and the race of beings upon whose salvation rests the fate of

civilization.

—. *The Einstein Intersection.* New York: Ace Books, 1967.

The story takes place in a far-distant future on Earth. Earth has been vacated by the human race and the time is so far in the future that it is a "world of romance." Into this world comes Lo Lobey, an alien, who tries to adapt to the bodies, the social forms and the life-styles of the Earth.

—. *Nova.* Garden City, New York: Doubleday, 1968.

Lord Von Ray battles the naked diabolism of Prince and Ruby Red, the unchallenged ruling force of Draco—a stellar complex which includes the earth and runs counter to Von Ray's federation of the Pleiades. In his quest for Illyrion which would make it possible for him to gain control of Draco, he involves several "wandering souls who preferred a meaningful chaos to the emptiness of order."

—. *The Fall of the Towers: A Classic Science Fiction Trilogy.* New York: Ace Books, 1972.

This is a compilation of the three books, *Captives of the Flame* (1963), *The Towers of Toron* (1964), and *City of a Thousand Suns* (1965). In this trilogy, the epic of Toromon unfolds on an Earth of fifteen hundred years or more into the future. Most of the planet has been destroyed by nuclear bombing; only fragmentary feudal states survive in livable pockets. Lord of the Flame, an extraterrestrial being who can destroy a world or hide in the soul of an insect and cannot be killed because he never lived, is attacking the Earth.

—. *Dhalgren.* New York: Bantam Books, 1974.

The story of Kid who cannot remember his name and wanders into a city called Bellona which has been struck by some undescribed disaster. Most of the population has gone. Kid gets involved progressively with a homosexual with a hoarding complex, a group living as a commune in the park with Lanya with a group of dropouts known as Scorpions and with various artistic people. Kid writes a book of poetry which is highly acclaimed. Then one day he is scared into leaving.

C. Allen, L. David. *Science Fiction Reader's Guide.* Lincoln, Nebraska: Centennial Press, 1974, pp. 215-218.

Babel-17 "depends on a state of science and technology that is advanced beyond the current state" in its "examination of the nature, characteristics, and results of an artificially-constructed language."

Barbour, Douglas. "Cultural Invention and Metaphor in the Novels of Samuel R. Delany." *Foundation: The Review of Science Fiction,* Numbers 7 and 8 (March 1975), 105-122.

A portion of Barbour's thesis is printed. Reproduced is the introduction, the section on the creation of fictional cultures by Delany, a brief section on Delany's style and a portion of the conclusion.

—. "Multiplex Misdemeanors: The Figures of the Artist and the Criminal in the SF Novels of Samuel R. Delany." *Khatru,* 2 May 1975, pp. 21-24, 60.

Delany constantly explores the theme of the artist and the criminal in his novels. He arrives at no answers about their value but does make the point that "the artistic consciousness differs from the merely criminal in its power of organization and control, it is creative—and multiplex—in a way the criminal consciousness can never be."

—. "Patterns of Meaning in the SF Novels of Ursula Le Guin, Joanna Russ and Samuel R. Delany, 1962-1972." Unpublished study at Queen's University, Kingston, Canada.

Chapter four explores Delany's "work under four headings: 'quest' [pattern] ...; figures of the artist and the criminal; cultural invention; and style." He attempts to show that "Delany is the best science-fiction writer in the world" and "one of the most interesting figures on the contemporary literary scene."

Blish, James, editor. *More Issues at Hand.* Chicago: Advent Publishers, Inc., 1970, pp. 134-136, 146.

Delany is good but not deserving of the acclaim he has received. However, he is an example of those who are revolutionizing science fiction.

Canary, Robert H. "Science Fiction as Fictive History." *Extrapolation: A Journal of Science Fiction and Fantasy,* 16 (December 1974), 81-95.

Delany's "*The Einstein Intersection* is...speculative fiction about our experience of history," not "what we accept as historical reality but operating by the same essential rules as that reality."

Delany, Samuel R. "About Five Thousand One Hundred and Seventy-Five Words." *Extrapolation: A Science Fiction Newsletter,* 10 (December 1968), 52-66.

"Put in opposition to 'style,' there is no such thing as content."

This article also appears in *SF: Essays on Modern Fantasy and Science Fiction,* edited by Thomas D. Clareson (Bowling Green, Ohio: Bowling Green University Popular Press, 1971).

—. "The Profession of Science Fiction: viii: Shadows— Part 1." *Foundation: The Review of Science Fiction,* Number 6 (May 1974), 31-60.

This "*is a theoretical statement which...applies very directly to science fiction...*[and] *open*[s] up some very large questions... about artistic creation and verbal communication."

—. "The Profession of Science Fiction: viii: Shadows— Part Two." *Foundation: The Review of Science Fiction,* Number 7 and 8 (March 1975), 122-154.

This *"is the second half of Chip Delany's* Shadows: *a 30,000 word treatise on words and meanings, a collage, a memoir, a manifesto, and incidentally, a statement about science fiction."*

—. "When Is a Paradox Not a Paradox?" *Foundation: The Review of Science Fiction*, Numbers 7 and 8 (March 1975), 100-102.

This *"belongs in* Shadow Part 1...*just after section 27...and the nature of reality."* Delany feels a "more formal analysis of the problem would be an appropriate addition."

—. "Critical Methods: Speculative Fiction." *Quark/No. 1.* New York: Paperback Library, 1970, pp. 182-195.

Serious Speculative Fiction criticism should examine a work in terms of its use of one or more of the mythic visions: New Jerusalem, Arcadia, The Land of Flies and Brave New World. "New Jerusalem and Brave New World are the only two new...[mythic views of the world] the twentieth century has produced."

Major, Clarence. "Clarence Major on New Fiction and Criticism." *Fiction International* 2/3 (1974), 151-154.

Delany sees the aim of speculative fiction as inventing reality.

Merril, Judith, editor. *S F 12.* New York: Dell, 1968, p. 381.

Biographical data on Delany is given.

Miesel, Sandra. "Samuel R. Delany's Use of Myth in 'Nova.'" *Extrapolation*, 12 (May 1971), 86-93.

Delany's ideas about myth are illustrated in *Nova*, a novel about power presented in the guise of the quest for the Holy Grail. His main myth is that "opposites are indispensable, for their interaction is the basis of all existence." In this work as in his other works, there is "a concern about the practice and theory of communication," the object of which is to reconcile opposites.

Samuelson, David. "New Wave, Old Ocean: A Comparative Study of Novels by Brunner and Delany." *Extrapolation,* 15 (December 1973), 75-96.

Delany's *The Einstein Intersection* as an example of " 'New Wave' " science fiction shows the broadening of the field. There is a use of symbols, an awareness that "hypothetical changes in technology or society are not the only lines...along which to extrapolate," a maintenance of the commercial pace and exotic flavor of popular adventure fiction and display of "moal toughness, artistic integrity, and awareness of a complex world of life and literature outside science fiction."

Scobie, Stephen. "Different Mazes: Mythology in Samuel R. Delaney's [sic] 'The Einstein Intersection.' " *Riverside Quarterly,* 5 (August 1972), 12-18.

He works with three distinct levels of myth: fictional, religious, and historical in presenting a future society. These "myths are images, not answers," and each individual who encounters them has to create his own pattern or response.

Smith, Jeffrey D. Review of *Driftglass* by Samuel R. Delany. *Phantasmicom,* September 1971, pp. 31-34.

"These ten stories, the product of his first three years in short fiction, are...distinctive, and alone will compensate for any number of small flaws."

D. *Babel-17*

Del Rey, Lester. Review of *Babel-17* by Samuel R. Delany. *Analog Science Fiction/Science Fact,* 80 (December 1967), 163-164.

This novel shows "how trivial and superficial a use of semantics" can be.

Samuel R. Delany

The Einstein Intersection

Del Rey, Lester. Review of *The Einstein Intersection* by Samuel R. Delany. *Analog Science Fiction/Science Fact,* 81 (April 1968), 163-164.

Ths novel "packs into itself enough tantalizing concepts,...color ...[and] insight for a whole shelf of books." In this book, he shows that the new science fiction writers are also "Renaissance men."

Nova

Gillam, Barry. "A Tune Beyond Us, Yet Ourselves: The *Nova* Notes." *SF Commentary* 14, August 1970, pp. 7-10.

The article examines *Nova*—a tightly structured novel—in terms of "points of interest, suggestions for lenses to view them through, corrections and replies to previous reviews." This novel "is examining the point at which a man meets his environment" and is "an updated Grail myth...[with a] theme equivalent to that of Wallace Stevens' THE MAN WITH THE BLUE GUITAR."

Dhalgren

Del Rey, Lester. Review of *Dhalgren* by Samuel R. Delany. *Analog Science Fiction/Science Fact,* 88 (May 1975), 170-172.

The novel is a "Whatisit," considered art, significant and relevant but it is "definitely *not* science fiction."

Jonas, Gerald. "S. F." *The New York Times Book Review,* 16 February 1975, pp. 27, 29-30.

This novel shows the coming of age of the genre. There is in this book no trace of science fiction's pulp origin," it is "genuine S. F. conceived and executed on...[a] level of sophisticaion. [It] may be the first S. F. novel wirtten with at least one eye on this new

S. F. audience—the students and professors of literature."

Last, Martin. Review of *Dhalgren* by Samuel R. Delany. *The Science Fiction Review,* 1 (March 1975), [8-9].

This "is something that few SF works are: it is highly personal, highly subjective and devoid of the familiar trappings of the genre." The possible theme "lies in the archetypal search for identity in an apathetic society." The novel is written "not to entertain, not to instruct and not to astound."

Lupoff, Richard. Review of *Dhalgren* by Samuel R. Delany. *Algol: A Magazine About Science Fiction,* Summer 1975, p. 29.

"It contains wonder, beauty, delight, boredom, tragedy, banality, art, vast gobbets of self-indulgence, self-doubt, self-praise, self-examination, self-deception, wish-fulfillment, possibly fear-fulfillment, reportage....It's incredibly rich, and very demanding of the reader."

WILLIAM DEMBY (1922—)

A. William Demby was born in Pittsburgh on December 25, 1922. He spent his World War II years in Italy. He graduated from Fisk University in 1947 and published his first book, *Beetlecreek,* in 1951. In 1947, he went to Italy to live and remained there until 1963 when he returned to America.

B. Demby, William. *The Catacombs.* New York: Pantheon, 1965.

Doris, a young girl living in Rome and employed as one of Eliza-beth Taylor's handmaidens in the filming of "Cleopatra," is having a novel written about her by a friend, William Demby—an expa-triate. The story spans 1961-1964, and, at the same time it depicts Doris' life, it explores many other events that are taking place in the world. Through this merger of Doris' life and current events, the author becomes revitalized, gains insight into himself and is able to return to the country of his birth as Black man and writer.

C. Bigsby, C. W. E. "From Protest to Paradox: The Black Writer at Mid Century." *The Fifties: Fiction, Poetry, Drama.* Edited by Warren French. Deland, Florida: Everett/Edwards, Inc., 1970, 224-226.

Demby's *Beetlecreek* is "a book which while ostensibly concerned with the plight of the Negro is in effect an inquiry into the plight of man in the modern world."

Bone, Robert. "William Demby's Dance of Live." *Tri Quarterly,* 15 (Spring 1969), 127-141.

The Catacombs is experimental but includes historical, biographical and fictional material. It can be approached through the conventional categories—setting, character and plot. His subject is the futility of man's imagination—man creates his own reality and in so doing demonstrates his reverence for life.

This article appears as the introduction to the Perennial Library edition of *The Catacombs.*

"Demby, William." *Living Black American Authors: A Biographical Directory.* Ann Allen Shocklev and Sue P. Chandler. New York: Bowker, 1973, p. 40.

Biographical data: birth, education, professional experience, memberships and publications.

Hoffman, Nancy Y. "The Annunciation of William Demby." *Studies in Black Literature,* 3 (Spring 1972), 8-13.

The Catacombs is an attestation that all is vital and sacramental. For Demby, the Black man and woman represent "human redemption." He affirms "possibility and salvation...and reconciliation and redemption in an age given to despair." He sees the role of woman as bearing life, both spiritual (love and physical).

—. "Techniques in Demby's *The Catacombs.*" *Studies in Black Literature*, 2 (Summer 1971), 10-13.

In *The Catacombs*, Demby juxtaposes old and new, uses a modified but highly personal form of the confessional, uses the story within the story, utilizes a collage effect, "develops his thought in sections of about the same length, all unified by a central axis," repeats images with an incremental purpose and uses a kind of circularity.

Johnson, Joe. "Interview with William Demby." *Black Creation*, 3 (Spring 1972), 18-21.

Demby discusses his creative process, his published novels and his projected novel. In *Beetlecreek*, he juxtaposes a man alone with a young boy growing up. In *The Catacombs*, he tries to establish a new way of looking at reality. In *The Journal of the Black Revolutionary in Exile*, his proposed novel, he is "experimenting with the concept of time and the many-faceted reality."

Margolies, Edward. "The Expatriate As Novelist: William Demby," *Native Sons: A Critical study of Twentieth Century Negro Authors.* Philadelphia: Lippincott, 1968, pp. 173-189.

William Demby, unlike most expatriate writers, has "a thoroughly unselfconscious immersion in European modes of thinking, conditioned by a profoundly American outlook." Both *Beetlecreek* and *The Catacombs* deal with death or evil and life or love and reason. He does not show the usual expatriate bitterness in his writing and is able to use his new environment.

Schraufnagel, Noel. *From Apology to Protest: The Black American Novel.* Deland, Florida: Everett/Edwards, Inc., 1973, pp. 128-129.

The Catacombs is the "story of the development of race in an American expatriate."

Singh, Raman K. "The Black Novel and Its Tradition." *Colorado Quarterly,* 20 (Summer 1971), 23-29.

The Catacombs is representative of the development of the major tradition in the Black novel. It presents the Identity-Quest in terms of success and it represents a rejection of the West and an acceptance of aspects of the Black heritage.

Walton, Martha R. Ballard. "Major Concerns of the Black Novel in America in Relation to the American Main-stream." Ph.D. dissertation, University of Denver, 1973, pp. 152-156.

Demby's *Beetlecreek* "is concerned with man" and universal human suffering. It is "a human document not an existentialist one."

Whitlow, Roger. *Black American Literature: A Critical History.* Chicago: Nelson Hall, 1973, pp. 122-125.

Biographical data and a discussion of Demby's first novel, *Beetle-creek,* which probes a "society gone dead."

"William Demby." *Interviews with Black Writers.* Edited by John O'Brien. New York: Liveright, 1973, pp. 35-53.

He is influenced by Virginia Woolf, Camus, Ellison, music, European films, science and Kierkegaard. He discusses his novels. He sees the obstacle to teaching and criticizing young Black writers as being age not race.

This interview appears in *Studies in Black Literature* for the Fall 1972.

D. *The Catacombs*

Buitenhuis, Peter. "Doris is Always Getting Pushed Aside." *The New York Times Book Review,* 11 July 1965, pp. 4, 32.

> *The Catacombs* is "not a novel but an autobiography, a pastiche or rag-bag." This is not to say Demby cannot write extremely well but that he did not in this book.

Winslow, Henry F., Sr. "Second Pitch." *Crisis,* 73 (January 1966), 57.

> This work is a montage which does not reach the height of his previous novel, *Beetlecreek.*

RONALD L. FAIR (1932—)

A. Ronald L. Fair was born in Chicago, Illinois, on October 27, 1932. He attended the Chicago public schools and business school. He has been a hospital corpsman in the United States Navy and a court reporter.

B. Fair, Ronald L. *Many Thousand Gone, An American Fable.* New York: Harcourt, 1965.

> Granny Jacobs, a resident in a small imaginary county in Mississippi where Black people are still held in slavery, manages the escape of her great grandson, Jesse. He is the son of the last pure Black in Jacobs County. He and Granny Jacobs communicate furtively through Preacher Harris, the only Black in the County who can read and write. She hears that Jesse has published a book and his

picture will appear in *Ebony*. She and the preacher decide to write the President and ask for help for the Blacks of Jacobs County. This brings chaos, strife and a sudden climax to the life in Jacobs County.

—. *Hog Butcher.* New York: Harcourt, 1966.

Ten-year-old Wilford Robinson and his pal, Earl of Chicago, witness the accidental shooting of their friend (Cornbread), an eighteen-year-old high school basketball star, by two policemen—one Black and one white. The neighborhood is incensed; a small riot erupts and the policemen are beaten. The police prepare a story for the inquest which is to whitewash them and degrade Cornbread. The two boys are the key witnesses. Wilford and his family are pressured to make him change his testimony.

—. *World of Nothing.* New York: Harper, 1970.

This book contains two novellas—*Jerome* and *World of Nothing*. Jerome is the bastard son of Father Jennings who plots to have Jerome put away because Jerome seems to accuse and unsettle him. The title novella, *World of Nothing,* is a first person narrative of life in the Chicago ghetto. The narrator and his friend Top live from one moment to the next.

—. *We Can't Breathe.* New York: Harper, 1971.

The story of Ernie Johnson growing up in the slums of Chicago in the thirties and forties. Ernie and his friends experience the destructive forces of white society. He, after serving as the leader of a street gang, grows into an awareness of his surroundings and their effect. He finally becomes a writer.

C. "Fair, Ronald." *Living Black American Authors: A Biographical Directory.* Ann Allen Shockley and Sue P. Chandler. New York: Bowker, 1973, p. 48.

Biographical data: birth, education, professional experience, awards, publications and address.

Fleming, Robert E. "The Novels of Ronald L. Fair." *CLA Journal*, 15 (June 1972), 477-487.

His "four published works reveal his ability to view black life from various perspectives—to perceive the comic as well as the tragic, the mythic as well as the trivial and commonplace." He utilizes a wide range of techniques and forms to convey his perceptions—fantasy, *Many Thousand Gone*; naturalism, *Hog Butcher* and *Jerome*; comic pictures, *World of Nothing.*

Klotman, Phyllis R. "The Passive Resistant in *A Different Drummer, Day of Absence* and *Many Thousand Gone.*" *Studies in Black Literature*, 3 (Autumn 1972), 7-11.

The Running Man is one of the Black writer's metaphors. Ronald Fair in *Many Thousand Gone* has three running men—Clay, Jesse, Little Jesse—but only one is later heard from. Running here is a subtle form of aggression, not a form of escape.

D. *Many Thousand Gone, An American Fable*

Tralis, Despi. "The Barbed Wire Rarely Shows." *Freedomways*, 5 (1965), 540-543.

This is "a requiem to the memory of the countless Negro victims of white supremacy whose collective breath scarcely ruffles a star or spoils the symmetry of a stripe on Old Glory."

Hog Butcher

Fuller, Hoyt W. Review of *Hog Butcher* by Ronald L. Fair. *Negro Digest*, 15 (October 1966), 84-86.

This illustrates what is good in the ghetto and is a portrayal of a specific diseased city which could be any American city.

Jones, John Henry. "Black Babbittry Dissected." *Freedomways*, 7 (1967), 87-88.

This is an honest book of the Black ghetto of Chicago whose only false note is the "happy ending."

We Can't Breathe

Bryant, Jerry H. "The Only Ground for Dignity." *The Nation,* 21 February 1972, pp. 253-254.

Ronald Fair should get more recognition for his careful and controlled craftsmanship. His ability attests to the mystery of the Black man's survival and maintenance of his humanity in America.

Davis, George. Review of *We Can't Breathe* by Ronald L. Fair. *The New York Times Book Review,* 6 February 1972, p. 6.

Review of a short, crisp and honest book which tells how nobly Black people have survived.

Johnson, Diane. Review of *We Can't Breathe* by Ronald L. Fair. *Book World,* 6 February 1972, p. 8.

The book "is curiously bland, devoid of drama and climax, like the lives it depicts" of Negroes born in the thirties to parents who had physically escaped the South.

LEON FORREST

B. Forrest, Leon. *There is a Tree More Ancient Than Eden.* New York: Random, 1973.

Nathan Witherspoon's life is recalled—his childhood and his junior high school days—during the funeral procession of young Nathan

Witherspoon's mother. At the same time, there is also a focus upon the deceased mother.

D. *There is a Tree More Ancient Than Eden*

Baker, Houston, Jr. "Two Views." *Black World,* 23 (January 1974), 66-69.

This is the work of a talented Black American and "an awe inspiring fusion of American cultural myth, Black American history, Black fundamentalist religion, the doctrine and dogma of Catholicism...and an autobiographical recall of days of anxiety and confusion..."

Gilbert, Zack. "Two Views." *Black World,* 23 (January 1974), 70.

This novel has the "moving and forceful...poetic flow" of Ellison's *Invisible Man.* However, the reviewer questions Forrest's intent as an artist, was he "writing only for the white literary establishment and a few pseudo Black intellectuals."

Hairston, Loyle. "Exceptional Fiction by Two Black Writers." *Freedomways,* 13 (1973), 337-340.

A book which has an unconventional, but effective style. It "informs both the mind and feeling of the spiritual richness of black life, celebrating those incidental uneventful moments that fill the space of a lifetime."

Davis, L. J. Review of *There is a Tree More Ancient Than Eden* by Leon Forrest. *The New York Times Book Review,* 21 October 1973, pp. 48-49.

The reviewer sees the book as being unclear and a bore.

ERNEST J. GAINES (1933—)

A. Ernest J. Gaines was born on a plantation in Oscar, Louisiana, January 15, 1931. In the late 1940's he moved to California. After high school and the army, he did his undergraduate work at San Francisco State College where he received his BA degree and did advanced study at Stanford University. He has received the Wallace Stegner Fellowship and the Joseph Henry Jackson Literary Award. He has published novels and short stories.

B. Gaines, Ernest J. *Of Love and Dust.* New York: Dial, 1967.

This is the story of Marcus who has killed a man in a roadhouse fight. He is bonded by Marshall Herbert to his feudal plantation. Bonbon, the overseer, tries to break Marcus' spirit. Marcus tries to seduce Bonbon's mistress. When she rebuffs him, he turns his attentions to Bonbon's wife. He wins her love and they plan to escape.

—. *A Long Day in November.* New York: Dial, 1971.

Sonny, the son of a cane-plantation worker in the early 1940's, recounts the events of one day in his life. On this day, his parents quarrel, separate, and finally become reconciled through the aid of Madam Toussaint.

—. *The Autobiography of Miss Jane Pittman.* New York: Dial, 1971.

A fictionalized account of a Black woman whose life spanned more than a century is recounted. Her story begins when she was a slave on a Louisiana plantation and freed because of the Emancipation Proclamation. She attempts to go to Ohio and freedom. She never reaches Ohio, but she spends her life in Louisiana and Texas in search of the "promised" freedom. The novel ends with her still moving towards freedom as she joins the freedom marchers.

C. Aubert, Alvin. "Gaines, Ernest J." *Contemporary Novelists.* Edited by James Vinson. New York: St. Martin's, 1972, pp. 444-446.

Biographical data, list of his publications, comments by Gaines and a brief discussion of Gaines as a writer who can be compared to William Faulkner and who creates notable characters both Black and white.

Billingsley, Ronald G. "The Burden of the Hero in Modern Afro-American Fiction." *Black World,* 25 (December 1975), 38-45, 66-73.

"In Gaines' work, we see that the price of re-definition always involves some willingness to suffer and often a willingness to risk death."

Bryant, Jerry H. "Ernest J. Gaines: Change, Growth and History." *The Southern Review,* 10 (October 1974), 851-864.

Gaines' earlier works were leading to *The Autobiography of Miss Jane Pittman* which fuses "the human and political implications of his subject," the old and the new. Miss Jane is optimistic, strong, durable, loyal, understanding and willing to fight. She is for her race and supports the dignity of her men and reinforces their courage. This is a historical novel which explores history and to Gaines this means characters—the little people, the ones who actually make history. Gaines' request in this novel as in all his novels is that we "respond to his characters as one human being to another" for "people are...fallible, perverse, contradictory...weak and strong, prudent and pig-headed, stubborn and too impressionable, likable and unlikable." The most important thing about his writing is "this generosity, this largeness of spirit."

—. "From Death to Life: The Fiction of Ernest J. Gaines." *The Iowa Review,* 3 (Winter 1972), 106-120.

> Gaines is seen maturing in his style and theme in his four books. The first two, *Catherine Carmier* and *Of Love and Dust,* are imitative in style of Hemingway and Faulkner. However, his third work, *Bloodline,* finds him acquiring and using his own voice which comes to full maturity in *The Autobiography of Miss Jane Pittman.* Similarly, the first two works show an ambivalence toward the rejection of the past or the future. However, in his third work he begins to develop the theme "that the present may work to make the future better than the past." By the fourth work, he has fully reconciled the past and present and sees them dependent upon each other for "out of death grows life." This forging of the new is dependent upon "the woman [who] preserves [and] the man [who] makes worthwhile what she preserves."

Carter, Tom. "Ernest Gaines." *Essence,* 6 (July 1975), 52-53, 71-72.

> The Black writer most to influence the writing of Gaines was Zora Neale Hurston. His life was influenced by his Aunt Augusten. It was because of the latter he developed his philosophy. One has to have a burden and to struggle; if he is knocked down, he keeps on getting up. He is now working on another book which is set in a Louisiana town after the death of Martin Luther King.

"Ernest J. Gaines." *Dark Symphony: Negro Literature in America.* Edited by James A. Emanuel and Theodore L. Gross. New York: Free Press, 1968, pp. 427-428.

> Biographical and critical statement and a brief discussion of "The Sky is Gray."

"Ernest J. Gaines." *Interviews With Black Writers.* Edited by John O'Brien. New York: Liveright, 1973, pp. 79-93.

Gaines was influenced by Russian writers and Greek tragedy. He attempts to examine "conflict between past and present, change and stasis" and the question of manhood. He sees death as necessary, not tragic. He discusses some aspects of each of his novels.

"Gaines, Ernest." *Black Writers Past and Present: A Biographical and Bibliographical Dictionary.* Theressa Gunnels Rush, Carol Fairbanks Myers, and Esther Spring Arata. Metuchen, New Jersey: The Scarecrow Press, Inc., 1975. I, 316-317.

Gaines' works and critical articles about him are listed.

"Gaines, Ernest J." *Contemporary Authors.* Edited by Clare D. Kinsmon and Mary Ann Tennenhouse. Detroit, Michigan: Gale Research Company, 1974. IX-XII, 311-312.

Biographical data: personal, career, writings, work in progress, sidelights, and critical sources.

Gayle, Addison, Jr. *The Way of the New World: The Black Novel in America.* Garden City, New York: Anchor/Doubleday, 1975, pp. 287-301.

Gaines "from his first novel *Catherine Carmier* (1964), to his latest, *The Autobiography of Miss Jane Pittman* (1971),...is concerned with specific elements of the racial past. Love, tragedy, interracial antagonisms,...rebellion...[and] that which takes precedence...is that men are circumscribed by historical patterns and that those who step outside such patterns are paradigms for future generations."

Gross, Robert A. "The Black Novelists: 'Our Time.' " *Newsweek,* 16 June 1969, pp. 94-98.

Ernest J. Gaines, a rather traditional writer, uses the rural South as his subject and his major theme is conflict between old and young.

Laney, Ruth. "A Conversation with Ernest Gaines." *The*

Ernest J. Gaines

Southern Review, 10 (January 1974), 1-14.

Gaines discusses his early life, his writing, technical aspects of *The Autobiography of Miss Jane Pittman,* his influences, writers of today, his philosophy, future work, political involvement and the responsibility of the writer. He feels the greatest thing to have happened to him was to be born in the South in the thirties, especially in Louisiana.

Ramsey, Alvin. "Through a Glass Whitely: The Televised Rape of Miss Jane Pittman." *Black World,* 23 (August 1974), 31-36.

"Instead of an honest dramatization of...Gaines' novel...we were offered the same ol' same ol'...the images and symbols" from the novel were distorted.

Schraufnagel, Noel. *From Apology to Protest: The Black American Novel.* Deland, Florida: Everett/Edwards, Inc., 1973, pp. 158-164.

Gaines' *Catherine Carmier* and *Of Love and Dust* "stress the point that racism stems largely from sexual fears."

Stoelting, Winifred L. "Human Dignity and Pride in the Novels of Ernest Gaines." *CLA Journal,* 14 (March 1971), 340-358.

"In the face of polarization, Gaines' characters demonstrate human dignity and pride." Gaines recognizes the need for change and the fact that his characters must make choices, but he is not concerned with the rightness of the choice, but with the dignity of the individual.

Williams, Sherley Anne. *Give Birth to Brightness/A Thematic Study of Neo-Black Literature.* New York: Dial, 1972, pp. 23, 27-29, 168-209, 218-222, 225, 226-228.

Gaines' concern is the effect of tradition on Black life. His main theme is the clash between old and new and young and old. For him, the secret to Black survival is Black love.   Discusses *Of Love and Dust*.

D. *Of Love and Dust*

Fuller, Hoyt W.   Review of *Of Love and Dust* by Ernest J. Gaines. *Negro Digest,* 17 (November 1967), 51-52, 85.

> The novel "deals honestly, and from a black viewpoint, with the commonplace but nonetheless 'delicate' sexual relationships prevalent in the *bayou* country."   The subject of the novel will insure its dismissal and neglect.

Lea, James. "A Door That Slavery Built." *Saturday Review,* 20 January 1968, p. 29.

> "He has written a book about Negroes and whites as just plain people, sharing equally the blame for maintaining a worn out tradition."

The Autobiography of Miss Jane Pittman

Bryant, Jerry H. "Politics and the Black Novel." *The Nation,* 5 April 1971, pp. 436-438.

> Gaines melds imaginative literature with political philosophy and speculation.   The success of this novel is due to Miss Jane, herself.

Dee, Ruby.   "Exciting Novel by Talented Story Teller." *Freedomways,* 11 (1971), 202-203.

> Miss Jane Pittman is a fictional character so well developed that the reader cannot believe she's an amalgamation of Black women and not one single individual.

Fuller, Hoyt W. Review of *The Autobiography of Miss Jane Pittman* by Ernest J. Gaines. *Black World,* 20 (October 1971), 87-89.

This book shows a Black woman who not only possesses strength and earthy wisdom but also remains "a simple, fallible, intensely human being."

Maddocks, Melvin. "Root and Branch." *Time,* 10 May 1971, pp. 98-117.

"This is not hot-and-breathless, burn-baby-burn writing." This is the work of a patient artist who watches and the revolution happens for him.

Major, Clarence. Review of *The Autobiography of Miss Jane Pittman. Essence,* 2 (September 1971), 8.

This is a novel which "achieves a level of strength and a love, steeped in historical experience, that is as impressive as his heroine's...stoical endurance and courage."

This review also appears in *Dark and Feeling* by Clarence Major.

Mellican, Arthenia Bates. Review of *The Autobiography of Miss Jane Pittman. CLA Journal,* 15 (September 1971), 95-96.

This is a novel which shows a woman as noble as an oak who "fixes her mind on an ideal to defy the pragmatic reality of a system which allowed men of lesser metal to excel only in inferiority."

Walker, Alice. Review of *The Autobiography of Miss Jane Pittman* by Ernest J. Gaines. *The New York Times Book Review,* 23 May 1971, pp. 6, 12.

He develops themes he has explored in his earlier works: dignity of man and the conflict between young and old.

Sam Greenlee

SAM GREENLEE (1930—)

A. Sam Greenlee was born in Chicago in 1930. He studied at the University of Wisconsin, University of Chicago and the University of Thessaloniki. He served with the United States Information Service in Iraq, Pakistan, Indonesia and Greece. He was officially honored for his activities during the 1958 Kassem revolution in Baghdad. In addition to his novels, he has written many articles and short stories.

B. Greenlee, Sam. *The Spook Who Sat by the Door.* New York: Richard W. Baron, 1969.

> The story of Don Freeman, a Black ex-gang leader, who lets the CIA teach him everything it knows about judo, guns, and strategy. He uses his knowledge to organize the gangs of Chicago into a crack guerrilla force and sends his lieutenants out to train the fighting gangs of every other ghetto city in the country, and turns snipers into marksmen, rioters into combat troops.

C. Burrell, Walter. "An Interview: Rappin With Sam Greenlee." *Black World,* 20 (July 1971), 42-47.

> Greenlee discusses his book, *The Spook Who Sat by the Door,* Black films, and the Black man's responsibility to himself and his people.

"Greenlee, Sam." *Living Black American Authors: A Biographical Directory.* Ann Allen Shockley and Sue P. Chandler. New York: Bowker, 1973, p. 62.

Biographical data: birth, education, family, professional experience, awards, publications, and address.

Gross, Robert A. "The Black Novelists: 'Our Time.' " *Newsweek,* 16 June 1969, pp. 94-98.

Greenlee says his novel is "about white faces and black masks."

Mason, B. J. "Sam Greenlee: A Player's Interview." *Players,* 2 (July 1975), 20-23.

Biographical data and a discussion of "white racist films in black face" and *The Spook Who Sat by the Door,* his reasons for writing it, its content and its publishing history.

Peavy, Charles D. "Four Black Revolutionary Novels, 1899-1970." *Journal of Black Studies,* 1 (December 1970), 219-223.

Greenlee's *The Spook Who Sat by the Door* is a handbook on how to succeed as a revolutionary and he sees confrontation between the races as unavoidable and the solution to America's race problem as annihilation.

Schraufnagel, Noel. *From Apology to Protest: The Black American Novel.* Deland, Florida: Everett/Edwards, Inc., 1973, pp. 191-195.

Greenlee's *The Spook Who Sat by the Door* "may be considered an outline of action for black militants, or a warning to white America about what the future holds if the general trends in the country continue."

Starke, Catherine Juanita. *Black Portraiture in American Fiction: Stock Characters, Archetypes, and Individuals.* New York: Basic Books, Inc., 1971, pp. 236-238.

Greenlee utilizes the Black avenger type in his novel, *The Spook Who Sat by the Door.*

D. *The Spook Who Sat by the Door*

Fuller, H. W. Review of *The Spook Who Sat by the Door* by Sam Greenlee. *Negro Digest*, 18 (May 1969), 73-74.

> Greenlee is to be commended for his introduction of "an authentic black hero," but his hero "does not breathe adequately as flesh and blood."

VIRGINIA HAMILTON (1936—)

A. Virginia Hamilton was born March 12, 1936 in Yellow Springs, Ohio. She now resides there with her husband and two children. She attended Antioch College, Ohio State University, and New School for Social Research. She has received numerous awards and honors for her books. In 1975, she became the first Black to receive the Newberry Award.

B. Hamilton, Virginia. *Zeely*. New York: Macmillan, 1967.

> The story of Elizabeth "Geeder" Perry and her brother, John "Toeboy" Perry, who spend a summer on their Uncle Ross' farm. Geeder dreams about Zeely—the tall, dark, handsome girl who tends the hogs on a part of Uncle Ross' farm. When Geeder finds a picture of a Watutsi queen, she decides Zeely must be a queen. Zeely has to bring Geeder back to reality.

—. *The House of Dies Drear*. New York: Macmillan, 1968.

> Thirteen-year-old Thomas Small, his father (a Civil War historian), his mother and brothers arrive at their new home in a small Ohio town. The house had been the home of Dies Drear, a murdered

abolitionist, and, since his death, had been empty because it was thought to be haunted. Thomas searches and discovers the secret of the house and more about the Underground Railroad. This is a mystery story.

—. *The Planet of Junior Brown.* New York: Macmillan, 1971.

The story of Junior Borwn—262 pounds, a compulsive eater and a music lover—and Buddy Clark—tall, quiet and a stand-in parent for a "planet" of homeless children. Junior Brown and Buddy Clark are eighth-graders who never go to class. They are aided in their class skipping by the janitor who, at one time, had been a school teacher. Junior Brown finally loses his grip on reality and is rescued by Buddy Clark and the school janitor.

—. *M. C. Higgins, the Great.* New York: Macmillan, 1974.

A few days in the life of Mayo Cornelius Higgins, a thirteen-year-old boy living in a small cabin with his family on a slope of Sarah's Mountain, are depicted. He sits atop his forty-foot steel pole and is able to see for miles. He sees and later encounters two strangers, the "dude" and Lurhetta; while atop his pole, he dreams of escape from the mountain.

C. Hamilton, Virginia. "High John Is Risen Again." *The Horn Book,* 51 (April 1975), 113-121.

High John de Conquer, the conqueror and trickster hero of slave stories, has returned. The acceptance of the sensibilities of the slave ancestors is the answer to alternatives to culturally prescribed ways of writing about Blacks and whites.

"Hamilton, Virginia." *Something About the Author,* Anne Commire. Detroit, Michigan: Gale Research Company, 1975. IV, 97-99.

Biographical data: personal, career, writings, works in progress, and a statement by Hamilton.

Hamilton, Virginia. "Newberry Award Acceptance." *The Horn Book,* 51 (August 1975), 337-343.

Discusses the background, problems and response of her hometown to her novel *M. C. Higgins, The Great.*

Heins, Paul. "Virginia Hamilton." *The Horn Book,* 51 (August 1975), 344-348.

Discusses Virginia Hamilton as a writer and a person. Biographical information is included.

Hopkins, Lee Bennett. *More Books by More People: Interviews with Sixty-five Authors of Books for Children.* New York: Citation Press, 1974, pp. 199-207.

Discussion of Hamilton's life, work and philosophy.

"Virginia Hamilton." *The Horn Book,* 48 (December 1972), 563-569.

Biographical data and comments on her books and characters.

Parks, Carole A. "Goodbye Black Sambo: Black Writers Forge New Images in Children's Literature." *Ebony,* 28 (November 1972), 60-70.

Hamilton attempts to write a "story kids can relate to...[and] to give information."

D. *The Planet of Junior Brown*

Giovanni, Nikki. Review of *The Planet of Junior Brown* by Virginia Hamilton. *Black World,* 21 (March 1972), 70-71.

This is a book which "could be a poem, or a prayer." It is about the middle class and the need "to live for each other."

Heins, Paul. Review of *The Planet of Junior Brown* by Virginia Hamilton. *The Horn Book,* 48 (February 1972), 81.

> Hamilton combines the "realism of detail and verisimilitude of speech with occasional touches of melodrama."

M. C. Higgins, The Great

Langston, Jane. "Virginia Hamilton, the Great." *The Horn Book,* 50 (December 1974), 671-673.

> Review of *M. C. Higgins, The Great,* a book in which Hamilton is like a "magician, or prestidigitator."

NATHAN C. HEARD (1936—)

A. Nathan C. Heard, novelist and teacher, was born in Newark, New Jersey, on November 17, 1936. He spent some time in jail where he began to read and to develop the desire to write. He has written three novels.

B. Heard, Nathan. *Howard Street.* New York: The Dial Press, 1968.

> The story of the relationship between Hip, a pimp and an addict, his brother Franchot and his girl Gypsy Pearl, the best prostitute on Howard Street. These and many minor characters are shown in their morality, honesty and acceptance of each other.

—. *To Reach a Dream.* New York: The Dial Press, 1972.

Bart Enos' one dream is to be as rich as the pimps and hustlers who are his idols. He goes to work for a wealthy Black widow knowing he will be able to manipulate her. However, he falls in love with the widow's daughter, Qurell. They become so obsessed with each other that they decide the only solution is to kill the mother.

—. *A Cold Fire Burning.* New York: Simon and Schuster, 1974.

Al, a young Black man living in Newark, tells of his affair with a white social worker named Terri. They meet when he saves her from being raped. Through this love-hate relationship, he attempts to come to grips with his racial identity.

C. "Nathan Heard." *Living Black American Authors: A Biographical Directory.* Ann Allen Shockley and Sue P. Chandler. New York: R. R. Bowker Comapny, 1973.

Biographical data: birth, education, family, professional experience, awards, publications and address.

Land, Irene Stokvis, editor. "First Novelists." *Library Journal,* 93 (October 1, 1968), 3585-3586.

Nathan Heard tells why and how he began to write.

D. *Howard Street*

Giovanni, Nikki. Review of *Howard Street* by Nathan Heard. *Negro Digest,* 18 (February 1969), 71-73.

The book is a "masterpiece" and another link in "classic Black literature" because of the "sheer technical skill and Black understanding."

Gross, Robert A. "The Black Novelists: 'Our Time.' " *Newsweek,* 16 June 1969, pp. 94-98.

Howard Street explores the search for identity and alternate values. Heard "explores a world devoid of middle-class illusions."

CHESTER HIMES (1909—)

A. Chester Himes was born of schoolteacher parents in Jefferson City, Missouri, in 1909 and educated at Ohio State University. He now lives in France. Himes spent time in the Ohio State Penitentiary where he witnessed and experienced a number of incidents which were to serve him in his writing. He has published five naturalistic novels, one satire and nine detective novels, at least one of which, *Cotton Comes to Harlem*, was made into a movie. He has also published two volumes of his autobiography.

B. Himes, Chester. *Cotton Comes to Harlem.* New York: Putman's Sons, 1965.

Detectives Grave Digger Jones and Coffin Ed Johnson along with Reverend Deke O'Malley and the white organization called Back-to-the-Southland search for $87,000 which has been swindled from the people of Harlem in a Back-to-Africa movement. The money is suspected of being in a bale of cotton.

—. *Pinktoes.* New York: Putnam, 1965.

Mamie Mason believes race relations can best be repaired in bed. She gives a series of parties and endeavors to obtain influential white persons for her gatherings and then they, Marie and the guests, proceed to work for reconciliation of the races.

—. *The Heat's On.* New York: G. P. Putnam's Sons, 1966.

A story of the dope racket in Harlem. The dope handlers and the police are trying to locate a $3,000 shipment of heroine that has come from France and is in Harlem.

—. *Run Man Run.* New York: G. P. Putman's Sons, 1966.

Walker, a white policeman with a brother-in-law on the New York police force, kills, without cause, two Negro workers and wounds another. The wounded man manages to escape and identifies Walker as his assailant. The story is an exploration of the dilemma of the hunted and the hunter when the picture is complicated by race.

—. *Blind Man with a Pistol.* New York: William Morrow and Company, 1969.

Coffin Ed and Grave Digger spend Nat Turner Day searching for the murderer of a white homosexual film producer. The day's search includes a demonstration for brotherhood and a protest for Black power. The novel points up the blindness of the inhabitants of Harlem.

C. Bennett, Stephen B. and William W. Nichols. "Violence in Afro-American Fiction: An Hypothesis." *Modern Fiction Studies,* 17 (Summer 1971), 221-228.

Chester Himes' *If He Hollers Let Him Go* explores the theme of creative violence.

Billingsley, Ronald G. "The Burden of the Hero in Modern Afro-American Fiction." *Black World,* 25 (December 1975), 38-45, 66-73.

"Perhaps nowhere in modern Black writing is the attempt of the hero to define and maintain himself as a positive and effective human being more poignantly revealed than in...*If He Hollers Let Him Go.*

Campenni, Frank J. "Black Cops and/or Robbers: The Detective Fiction of Chester Himes." *The Armchair Detective,* 8 (May 1975), 206-209.

Himes turns the detective novel upside down for the conventions do not fit—anything can happen in Harlem, an absurd place. "There is no justice to restore, no order to resume, no relevance to logic." Here, the cops will "shake you down or shake you up,... they can break the law with impunity."

Chelminski, Rudolph. " 'Cotton' Cashes in." *Life,* 69 (August 28, 1970), 59-61.

Discusses the background which spawned Himes' novel and later the movie *Cotton Comes to Harlem.*

Dance, Daryl Cumber. "Wit and Humor in Black American Literature." Ph.D. dissertation, University of Virginia, 1971.

"Himes' later works, such as *Pinktoes, Blind Man with a Pistol* and *Cotton Comes to Harlem* rely for their humor on numerous wild sexual encounters, obscene language, ribald jokes and all kinds of buffunery and slapstick...." Himes "is known for his wildly comic farces characterized by bawdiness and ribaldry...."

Davis, Arthur P. "Chester Himes." *From the Dark Tower: Afro-American Writers 1900 to 1960.* Washington, DC: Howard University Press, 1974, pp. 162-167.

Himes' writing falls into two phases. The first, 1947-1955, is marked by the publication of "five novels influenced by the Richard Wright school of thought, naturalistic writing." The second phase, 1957, to the present, is marked by the publication of *Pinktoes,* a satire on sex and race relations, a series of detective stories, which were not as well received in America as in France, and an autobiography.

Fabre, Michel. *"A Case of Rape." Black World,* 21 (March 1972), 39-43.

A Case of Rape "remains without a doubt...[Himes'] most mysterious novel." This novel sheds "light on racism in France and... allows us to grasp some essential motifs in [his]...work and to better understand how he manages to transform historical events into imaginary episodes."

—. "Chester Himes' Published Works: A Tentative Check List." *Black World,* 21 (March 1972), 76-78.

Listed are Himes' novels, short stories, non fiction and some critical articles about him.

Fuller, Hoyt W. "Traveler on the Long, Rough, Lonely Old Road: An Interview with Chester Himes." *Black World,* 21 (March 1972), 4-22, 87-98.

An interview "published on the occasion of the publication of Part One of his autobiography, *The Quality of Hurt.*" Himes discusses his works, his problems with publishers, the reception of his works, Black and white critics and wirters: young Blacks, Ellison, Baldwin and Wright.

Gayle, Addison, Jr. *The Way of the New World: The Black Novel in America.* Garden City, New York: Anchor Press/Doubleday, 1975, pp. 181-191.

Himes "shared Wright's belief in the stunting, limiting capabilities of environment" but was himself an innovator in character delineation. He showed rage, hostility, fear and enmity to be universal within the Black psyche, poor and middle class, in his novels, *If He Hollers Let Him Go* and *The Lonely Crusade.*

Greenlee, Sam. Review of *The Quality of Hurt* by Chester Himes, *Black Books Bulletin,* 1 (Spring/Summer 1972), 52-57.

This review uses excerpts from the book to tell of Himes—a fatalist in the Eastern sense, a saddened but seldom bitter man, a scarred but uncrippled man. The "essence of...Himes is in his work," the novels.

Hill, James Lee. "Bibliography of the Works of Chester Himes, Ann Petry and Frank Yerby." *Black Books Bulletin,* 3 (Fall 1975), 60-72.

Lists Himes' works and biographical and critical writings about him. Some of the secondary sources are annotated.

Himes, Chester. "Dilemma of the Negro Novelist in the U.S.A." *New Black Voices: An Anthology of Contemporary Afro-American Literature.* Edited by Abraham Chapman. New York: Mentor Books, 1972, pp. 394-401.

The Negro writer is in conflict with himself, his public and his environment. He must decide how honest he is going to be in his writing and accept the fact that change is inevitable. He must also cease to hate the faces of white and instead hate the evil. This is his service as an artist.

This essay also appears in *Beyond the Angry Black.* Edited by John A. Williams (New York: Cooper Square Publishers, 1966).

—. *The Quality of Hurt: The Autobiography of Chester Himes.* Volume I. New York: Doubleday, 1971.

The facts of Himes' life up to his mid-forties appear in this book.

"Himes, Chester." *Black American Writers Past and Present: A Biographical and Bibliographical Dictionary.* Theressa Gunnels Rush, Carol Fairbanks Myers and Esther Spring Arata. Metuchen, New Jersey: The Scarecrow Press, Inc., 1975. I, 380-383.

Biographical data and works by and about him are listed.

"Himes, Chester." *Contemporary Authors.* Edited by Carolyn Riley. Detroit, Michigan: Gale Research Company, 1971. XXV-XXVIII, 343-344.

Biographical data: personal, career, writings, work in progress, sidelights, and biographical/critical sources.

"Himes, Chester." *Contemporary Literary Criticism.* Edited by Carolyn Riley and Barbara Harte. Detroit, Michigan: Gale Research Company, 1974. II, 194-196.

Critical statements on *Blind Man with a Pistol, A Case of Rape, The Quality of Hurt* and his detective fiction.

Kane, Patricia and Doris Y. Wilkinson. "Survival Strategies: Black Women in *Ollie Miss* and *Cotton Comes to Harlem.*" *Critique,* 16, Number 1, pp. 101-109.

Iris, a minor character in *Cotton Comes to Harlem,* does not suffer from the general treatment of the Black woman in American literature. She "refuses to accept defeat and transcends the potentially crippling identity her situation invites."

Klotman, Phyllis R. "The White Bitch Archetype in Contemporary Black Fiction." *Bulletin of the Midwest Modern Language Assocaition,* 6 (Spring 1973), 96-110.

"Madge, the Texas cracker in Himes' novel [*If He Hollers, Let Him Go*], thrives on the notion that blacks are savage and sexually aggressive."

Margolies, Edward. "Experiences of the Black Expatriate Writer: Chester Himes." *CLA Journal,* 15 (June 1972), 421-427.

Himes' expatriate experiences have made him very pessimistic. He has been unable to assimilate his European experiences into his writing; his best writing is in his detective novels. His novels no longer contain a protest tone.

—. "Race and Sex: The Novels of Chester Himes." *Native Sons: A Critical Study of Twentieth Century Negro Authors.* Philadelphia: J. B. Lippincott Company, 1968, pp. 87-101.

Himes' protagonists are generally fairly well educated, middle class, somewhat sophisticated and articulate. His themes are bigotry, violence, emasculation and sexual insecurity of the white male. Margolies examines these themes and the protagonists in *The Third Generation, If He Hollers Let Him Go, Lonely Crusade, The Primitive* and *Pinktoes.*

—. "The Thrillers of Chester Himes." *Studies in Black Literature,* 1 (Summer 1970), 1-11.

Himes like Dashiell Hammett writes from experience, sees American cities as corrupt and has some faith in a moral order. However, his stance is different from Hammett's. He, by the use of humor: like the slapstick of the Keystone Cops, is able to laugh at violence. He "carries the dime detective format to its logical absurdity." His focus is on man's venality rather than his virtue. His "violent comedies are a commentary on the...nature of American life."

Mok, Michael. "PW Interviews: Chester Himes." *Publishers Weekly,* 201 (April 3, 1972), 20-21.

Himes says he takes his "stories from the Black Experience as...[he has] undergone it."

Nelson, Raymond. "Domestic Harlem: The Detective Fiction of Chester Himes." *The Virginia Quarterly Review,* 48 (Spring 1972), 260-276.

The Harlem Domestic Series, novels about two Harlem police detectives: Coffin Ed Johnson and Grave Digger Jones, present a variety of character types, grotesque style and popular crime formulae. The five novels written between 1958 and 1961 are not only classic detective stories but are also an "imaginative history of the changing social and psychological orientation of Black Americans."

Reed, Ishmael. "Chester Himes: Writer." *Black World,* 21 (March 1972), 23-38, 83-86.

Reed discusses Himes' works and his life. He concludes that Himes, the poet, folklorist and critic, is, in spite of "the sheer hatred directed at him by everybody," still "his cantankerous, irascible, feisty, brilliant self." He has a lengthy discussion of *The Quality of Hurt.*

Reilly, John M. "Himes, Chester (Bomar)." *Contemporary Novelists.* Edited by James Vinson. New York: St. Martin's Press, 1972, pp. 611-613.

Biographical data, list of publications and a discussion of his work and its intent: show the "relationship between social environment and individual personality."

Starke, Catherine Juanita. *Black Portraiture in American Fiction: Stock Characters, Archetypes and Individuals.* New York: Basic Books, Inc., 1971, pp. 77-81.

Himes' characters have a superficial resemblance to the earlier buffoons. However, on closer examination one realizes "Himes delineates a broad spectrum of black characters which may more accurately be classified as Harlem grotesques combining caricatured appearances and motives with nightmare-like situations and sequences."

Thompson, M. Cordell. "Chester Himes: Portrait of an Expatriate." *Jet,* 42 (June 8, 1972), 28-30.

Discussion of Himes as a writer and his relationship with Richard Wright is mentioned.

Williams, John A. "My Man Himes: An Interview with Chester Himes." *Amistad 1.* Edited by John A. Williams and Charles F. Harris. New York: Vintage Books, 1970, pp. 25-91.

Himes discusses publishing, writing, writers and his life.

D. *Cotton Comes to Harlem*

"Baleful of Laughs," *The Times Literary Supplement,* 20 January 1966, p. 37.

Even though *Cotton Comes to Harlem* has a "laugh on nearly every page," it is still apparent Himes is Black and concerned about his people's plight.

Blind Man With a Pistol

Boyd, Melba J. Review of *Blind Man with a Pistol* by Chester Himes. *Black World,* 21 (March 1972), 51-52, 68-69.

An "attempt to examine the personalities of Harlem" by showing "the blindness of Black people to their pitiful existence, and how they got there."

Margolies, Edward. "America's Dark Pessimism." *Saturday Review,* 22 March 1969, pp. 69, 64-65.

This is an exceedingly American book in its treatment of racism and violence.

Rhodes, Richard. Review of *Blind Man with a Pistol* by Chester Himes. *The New York Times Book Review,* 23 February 1969, p. 32.

Himes' paternalistic attitude toward his characters supports the assertion that he is prejudiced. The view expressed is one not unlike a white man's view of Harlem.

Stevens, Shane. Review of *Blind Man with a Pistol* by Chester Himes. *Book World,* 27 April 1969, pp. 4-5.

Himes who has created a series of interlocking people "as fully formed as Faulkner's...Yoknapatawpha County" may be "the best contemporary American practitioner of the lost art of narration."

KRISTIN HUNTER (1931—)

A. Kristin Hunter—lecturer, teacher, novelist, short story writer—was born in Philadelphia, Pennsylvania, on September 12, 1931. She attended the University of Pennsylvania. She has received a Whitney Fellowship, the Sigma Delta Chi award for reporting, and the National Council on Interracial Books for Children Award.

B. Hunter, Kristin. *The Landlord.* New York: Scribners, 1966.

> Edgar Enders, a young white man, is handsome, wealthy, and neurotic. He has a desperate need to find the love, identity and sense of usefulness he has never had in his own family. He buys an apartment building and becomes a landlord. He finds his tenants are Black, but determines to make these people his family.

—. *The Soul Brothers and Sister Lou.* New York: Scribner, 1968.

> The story of Louretta Hawkins (Sister Lou), a fourteen-year-old Black girl living in a five-room house with her mother, her eight brothers and sisters and her older sister's illegitimate baby is told. The story demonstrates Sister Lou's maturation and discovery of her Black identity through struggling and suffering.

—. *The Survivors.* New York: Scribners, 1975.

> Miss Lena Ricks, middle-aged owner and operator of a dress shop, accepts the help of B. J., a thirteen-year-old crippled boy, who runs errands and cleans for her. She becomes very dependent on and involved with him. She becomes so involved that she begins to know

about his private life—his running with a bad crowd, his drinking and abusive father and later his part in a robbery of her store.

C. "Hunter, Kristin (Mrs. John I. Lattany)." *Black American Writers Past and Present: A Biographical and Bibliographical Dictionary.* Theressa Gunnels Rush, Carol Fairbanks Myers and Esther Spring Arata. Metuchen, New Jersey: The Scarecrow Press, Inc., 1975. I, 403-404.

Biographical data, photograph, and a list of "all known published books."

"Hunter, Kristin (Eggleston)." *Contemporary Authors.* Edited by James M. Ethridge and Barbara Kopala. Detroit, Michigan: Gale Research Company, 1965. XIII-XIV, 223.

Biographical data: personal, career, writings, work in progress and sidelights.

Reilly, John M. "Hunter, Kristin." *Contemporary Novelists.* Edited by James Vinson. New York: St. Martin's, 1972, pp. 653-655.

Biographical data, publications, and a discussion of *God Bless the Child, The Landlord* and *The Soul Brothers and Sister Lou* are contained in this article. Her works seek to show "a contradiction between reality and assumptions carried by familiar popular fiction."

Schraufnagel, Noel. *From Apology to Protest: The Black American Novel.* Deland, Florida: Everett/Edwards, Inc., 1973, pp. 141-144.

Hunter's novels are in the accommodationist vein—quest for a racial identity which allows the characters to function in the mainstream.

Whitlow, Roger. *Black American Literature: A Critical*

History. Chicago: Nelson Hall, 1973, pp. 151-154.

Biographical data and a discussion of *The Landlord* as satire.

D. *The Landlord*

Sarris, Andrew. "Good Intentions." *The New York Times Book Review,* 24 April 1966, p. 41.

The novel demonstrates "an act of emotional restraint, a triumph of form over feeling." However, readers are apt to be disappointed at the "relatively urbane view of race relations."

The Soul Brothers and Sister Lou

Bond, Jean Carey. "Disappointing Novel for Teen-Agers." *Freedomways,* 9 (1969), 273-276.

The novel fills an enormous need in teen-age fiction but is marred by its "tone of condescension" and stereotypical treatment of color. However, it is "stylistically persuasive."

The Survivors

Blakely, Henry. Review of *The Survivors* by Kristin Hunter. *Black Books Bulletin,* 3 (Fall 1975), 31, 34.

"In its best moments it has charm, a fey quality, a trace of fantasy running through it like fine gold threads in lamé cloth." However, "it comfortably reinforces stereotypes" and thus the author "has used a powerful tool dangerously."

BLYDEN JACKSON

A. Blyden Jackson was born in New Haven, Connecticut. He completed his education in the United States Marine Corps and at New York University. He has worked as a baker, truck driver, messenger, rent-a-car agent, and printer. He is the author of *American Economic Involvement in South Africa.*

B. Jackson, Blyden. *Operation Burning Candle.* New York: Third Press, 1973.

> Aaron Rogers, a brilliant student in medicine and psychology, gives up his studies and volunteers for Vietnam. His family receives a notice of his death in Vietnam, but while they await his body, one of the family sees a man like him. At the same time, banks are being raided, informers are being killed, false alarms are being turned on and subways halted. The police suspect a new, well trained group. The group turns out to be comprised of presumably dead Black Vietnam veterans led by Aaron Rogers. They are able to execute their mission, "Operation Burning Candle," during a Democratic Convention at Madison Square Garden.

—. *Totem.* New York: Third Press, 1974.

> A totem statue, from pre-colonial Africa and a potent symbol of Africa, has long disappeared. A New York Black commissions some young Black compatriots to find and return it to the African people.

D. *Operation Burning Candle*

Bryant, Jerry H. "The Outskirts of a New City." *The Nation,* 12 November 1973, pp. 501-502, 504.

> "A very readable novel, slickly organized, with violence, sex and propaganda occurring in just the right rhythm."

JESSE JACKSON (1908—)

A. Jesse Jackson was born in Columbus, Ohio, on January 1, 1908. He attended Ohio State University and has been a professional boxer. He has worked as a writer and lecturer and served as visiting associate professor at Appalachian State University. He won the Child Study Association's Award for his first book, *Call Me Charley* which was written in 1945.

B. Jackson, Jesse. *Tessie.* New York: Harper, 1968.

> This is the story of Tessie Downs who wins a scholarship to Hobbe, an exclusive private school in Manhattan. Her mother is against her accepting it because it will mean she will have a hard time making friends, maintaining her place at home in Harlem and meeting the scholastic standards. Tessie is able to reconcile these worlds— home and Hobbe.

—. *The Sickest Don't Always Die the Quickest.* New York: Doubleday, 1971.

> The story of twelve-year-old Stonewall Jackson who is a confirmed sinner troubled by three questions. Would Aunt Hettie, the only

91

one in the family who seems to love and understand him, believe the rumors which were circulating about him? Would he drown when he was baptized and take the one-way road to heaven? Would he fail his TB test and have to return to the sanitarium? The story tells how the questions were answered and what he learns.

Jackson, Jesse. *The Fourteenth Cadillac.* New York: Doubleday, 1972.

The story of Stonewall Jackson, a seventeen-year-old high school drop out, is told. He is in trouble because his Aunt Hettie is dead, he cannot find a job and refuses to take the only one available, undertaker. He gets a job on a horse farm and later decides the only way to survive is to leave home, but this will make people unhappy.

C. "Jackson, Jesse." *Black American Writers Past and Present: A Biographical and Bibliographical Dictionary.* Theressa Gunnels Rush, Carol Fairbanks Myers, and Esther Spring Arata. Metuchen, New Jersey: Scarecrow Press, Inc., 1975. II, 414-415.

Biographical statement, photograph, and a list of "all known published books."

"Jackson, Jesse." *Contemporary Authors.* Edited by Carolyn Riley. Detroit, Michigan: Gale Research Company, 1971. XXV-XXVIII, 373.

Biographical data: personal, career and writing.

"Jackson, Jesse." *Something About the Author.* Anne Commire. Detroit, Michigan: Gale Research Company, 1975. II, 150-152.

Biographical data: personal, career, writings, sidelights, photograph and sources of additional information.

Parks, Carole A. "Goodby Black Sambo: Black Writers Forge New Images in Children's Literature." *Ebony,* 28 (November 1971).

> Jackson says his writing of children's books grew out of his "experiences as a probation officer."

D. *Tessie*

Birmingham, Mary Louise. Review of *Tessie* by Jesse Jackson. *The New York Times Book Review,* 26 May 1968), p. 30.

> "This is a bloodless drawing-room tragicomedy, even narrower than 'Guess Who's Coming to Dinner.' "

The Sickest Don't Always Die the Quickest

Zoss, Betty. Review of *The Sickest Don't Always Die the Quickest* by Jesse Jackson. *The New York Times Book Review,* 14 February 1971, p. 20.

> "TSDADTQ is fresh, warm, honest Americana about a real American boy."

CHARLES JOHNSON (1948—)

A. Charles Johnson was born in 1948. He worked with cartoonist Lawrence Lariar and later worked as a cartoonist and comic book writer, as an editorial cartoonist and reporter and published over 1000 drawings. His work has been collected and published in one volume—*Black Humor.* He created, hosted and co-produced an educational television series called, "Charlie's Pad." He attended Southern Illinois University and is pursuing the Ph.D. degree at the State University of New York at Stony Brook.

B. Johnson, Charles. *Faith and the Good Thing.* New York: Viking, 1974.

> Faith Cross, the main character, is an eighteen-year-old girl from rural Georgia. She is an innocent who travels to Chicago after listening to her mother's deathbed advice to look for the "Good Thing." She becomes a whore, a housewife, an adultress. She bears a child, dies in a fire, but lives again.

C. "First Novelists." *Library Journal,* 99 (October 1, 1974), 2508.

> Johnson tells of his background, his novel which operates "on three levels—fantasy, realism, and allegory," and his ideas on fiction.

D. *Faith and the Good Thing*

Cash, Earl A. Review of *Faith and the Good Thing* by Charles Johnson. *Black World,* 24 (August 1975), 92-95.

> Johnson has written a novel which demonstrates "that Blacks are still capable of novels which combine the particular problems of race with the universal crises of mankind, while sacrificing nothing in the area of stlyle and form." As a result of this novel, Johnson has a burden "akin to that which *Invisible Man* placed on Ralph Ellison."

Simpson, Janice C. Review of *Faith and the Good Thing* by Charles Johnson. *Essence,* 6 (October 1975), 44.

> "This is not an easy book to read...but...Johnson is...a storyteller."

Thus, the senses and the intellect are involved simultaneously.

Smith, Barbara. "Seeking 'Good Thing,' Faith Finds it in Herself." *The National Observer,* 9 November 1974, p. 25.

> This novel "combines elements of folk fable, melodrama and philosophical quest...Johnson takes the well worn theme of the search for identity, meaning, and love and conjures it into something rich and strange and extremely gratifying."

Yvonne. "Pain and Fancy." *Ms,* 4 (August 1975), 43-44.

> "Perhaps this novel *is* novel—a Negro search for the Holy Grail... but I think this book a subversive kink."

GAYL JONES (1949–)

A. Gayle Jones was born in Lexington, Kentucky, on November 23, 1949. She attended Connecticut College and Brown University. She has won the Frances Steloff Award for fiction, the Shubert Foundation Grant for playwriting and a scholarship to Breadloaf Writers Conference.

B. Jones, Gayl. *Corregidora.* New York: Random, 1975.

> Ursa Corregidora, a Black cafe singer, is the last of three generations of Corregidora women. The Corregidora women are the progeny of Corregidora, the Portuguese who fathered his own slaves, his own concubines and his own prostitutes. Ursa is the only one with a different father. Yet, she is haunted by her past and the fact that she cannot live up to the responsibility demanded

of her by the three generations of Corregidora women who preceded her: to "make generations."

C. "Gayl Jones." *People,* 9 June 1975, p. 69.

Photograph and a brief biographical statement.

"Jones, Gayl." *Black Writers Past and Present: A Biographical and Bibliographical Dictionary.* Theressa Gunnells Rush, Carol Fairbanks Myers, and Esther Spring Arata. Metuchen, New Jersey: The Scarecrow Press, Inc., 1975. II, 439-440.

Biographical statement, photograph, list of her known works and a statement by Jones.

D. *Corregidora*

Darden, Norman. Review of *Corregidora* by Gayl Jones. *Encore,* 21 July 1975, p. 41.

Jones has talent, but "technical deficiencies as a novelist"; hopefully she is at work "on another novel to prove, with greater technical proficiency, the obvious—that she can write and tell a story."

Jefferson, Margo. "Making Generations." *Newsweek,* 19 May 1975, pp. 84-85.

"Gayle Jones' first novel, 'Corregidora,' is a gripping portrait of... [the] harsh sexual and psychological genealogy" of the Black "slave women who were mistress and breeder to their white owners."

Larson, Charles R. "Jones." *The National Observer,* 9 August 1975, p. 17.

This is "a novel...hammered from our common transgressions."

She "shares a number of themes" with Faulkner. It "is a remarkable achievement" which feels not like a novel but oral history.

Pochoda, Elizabeth. Review of *Corregidora* by Gayl Jones. *Glamour*, 73 (September 1975), 97.

Corregidora "manages to retell Faulkner's *Go Down, Moses* from a black perspective."

Review of *Corregidora* by Gayl Jones. *Black Books Bulletin*, 3 (Fall 1975), 46-47.

"Gayl Jones has demonstrated a maturity of style and depth of insight that gives evidence of a significant literary figure in the making."

Sokolov, Raymond. Review of *Corregidora* by Gayl Jones. *The New York Times Book Review*, 25 May 1975, pp. 21-22.

Her "interior monologue [is] so natural it seems almost crude to say she is using the stream-of-consciousness technique." There is a distinct contrast "between Joyce's self-conscious experimentalism and Gayl Jones's nonchalance." Her novel is too short, but it raises expectations and desires for more.

Webster, Ivan. "Really the Blues." *Time*, 16 June 1975, p. 79.

If *Corregidora* did not "illuminat the wider question of the way all men need women, it could be written off as pulp melodrama. Not "since Richard Wright's Native Son (1940) has [a Black American writer] so skillfully traced psychic wounds to a sexual source."

JUNE JORDAN (1936—)

A. June Jordan was born in New York, New York, on July 9, 1936   She attended Northfield School, Barnard College and the University of Chicago.   She has worked as both teacher and lecturer.   She has won the Rockefeller grant for Creative Writing and the Prize of Rome in Environmental Design. She is a poet, article writer and novelist.

B. Jordan, June.   *His Own Where.*   New York: T. Crowell, 1971.

> This is the story of fourteen-year-old Angela and sixteen-year-old Buddy who have to create their own "where" in order to survive. Buddy's father is in a hospital dying and Angela, his only other love, has been beaten and later sent to a shelter. She gets a weekend pass and goes to Buddy.   They move to an empty house near a cemetery where their love will be the refuge and hope that will save them.

C. Bragg, Pamela.   "PW Interviews: June Jordan."   *Publishers' Weekly,* 21 February 1972, pp. 60-61.

> She discusses her interests, her novel *His Own Where* and her beliefs about man, ghettos and Black English.

"Jordan, June."   *Black American Writers Past and Present: A Biographical and Bibliographical Dictionary.*   Theressa Gunnels Rush, Carol Fairbanks Myers and Esther Spring Arata.   Metuchen, New Jersey: The Scarecrow Press, Inc., 1975.   II, 446-447.

Biographical data is given and all known works are listed.

"Jordan, June." *Contemporary Authors.* Edited by Clare D. Kinsman and Mary Ann Tennenhouse. Detroit, Michigan: Gale Research Company, 1973. XXXIII-XXXVI, 485-486.

Biographical data: personal, career, awards and honors, writings and biographical/critical sources.

Jordan, June. "Young People: Victims of Realism in Books and in Life." *Wilson Library Bulletin*, 48 (October 1973), 142-143.

Jordan's manifesto is to devise reasonable alternatives to the negative reality that "consigns us to frustration, shame, and impotence" and to "offer these alternatives particularly to young readers." Realism must be redefined to include an end to atrocity and the beginning of a new worldwide situation" in which victims become active.

Parks, Carole A. "Goodbye Black Sambo: Black Writers Forge New Images in Children's Literature." *Ebony*, 28 (November 1972), 60-70.

Discusses Miss Jordan's reaction to the word *Negro* and her first book *Who Look at Me.*

WILLIAM MELVIN KELLEY (1937—)

A. William Melvin Kelley was born in New York City in 1937. He attended Fieldstone School in New York and Harvard. He studied under John Hawkes and Archibald MacLeish. He has won the Dana Reed Literary Prize and the Rosenthal Foundation award of the National Institute of Arts and Letters.

B. Kelley, William Melvin. *A Drop of Patience.* Garden City, New York: Doubleday, 1965.

This is the story of Ludlow Washington, a blind Black musician. He was placed in a home when he was five because his father was unable to cope with a blind child. He did so well at music a band leader took Ludlow out of the home when he was sixteen and gave him a chance to play with a band. This, then, is the story of his fight from the bottom to make a living as a musician.

—. *dem.* Garden City, New York: Doubleday, 1967.

A satire on American society. The book explores the mind of Mitchell Pierce, a Madison Avenue advertising executive, whose wife, Tam, gives birth to fraternal twins—one Black and one white. Pierce sets out to find the Black father and in his search Kelly draws a portrait of American society and its problems.

—. *Dunfords Travels Everywhere.* Garden City, New York: Doubleday, 1969.

The story pursues Craig Dunford, a Black American, and a group of white Americans through a fictitious country in Europe. Carlyle Bedlow, a Harlem conman, also is portrayed.

C. Abraham, Willie E. "Introduction." *dem.* William Melvin Kelley. New York: Collier Books, 1969, pp. vii-xii.

"*dem* is...raceless," it passes no judgment on the race issue. Kelley suggests the way to rise from the Orwellian society which already exists is "to claim a common lot for the black man with everyone else in American society."

Anderson, Jervis. "Black Writing: The Other Side." *Dissent,*

15 (May-June 1968), 233-242.

Kelley's focus on life shifts with his novel *dem*. He now preaches separatism.

Beards, Richard. " 'Parody as Tribute: William Melvin Kelley's *A Different Drummer* and Faulkner.' " *Studies in Black Literature,* 5 (Winter 1974), 25-28.

Kelley is indebted to Faulkner in characterization, tone, narrative method, yet he does not merely imitate. He "insists that the South will arrive at a transcendent and Edenic dream rather than perish in a Snopseian nightmare."

Borden, William. "Kelley, William Melvin." *Contemporary Novelists.* Edited by James Vinson. New York: St. Martin's, 1972, pp. 708-709.

Biographical data, a list of his publications and a discussion of his novels—*A Different Drummer, A Drop of Patience* and *dem.*

Dance, Daryl Cumber. "Wit and Humor in Black American Literature." Ph.D. dissertation, University of Virginia, 1971.

William Melvin Kelley is one of the authors Dance uses to develop her idea that Black humor which is rooted in folklore and follows an established tradition "lacks positive aspects and optimism" in contemporary literature.

Gayle, Addison, Jr. *The Way of the New World: The Black Novel in America.* Garden City, New York: Anchor Press/Doubleday, 1975, pp. 302-310.

Kelley in *A Different Drummer* and *Dunsfords Travels Everywhere* "has opted...for literature which deals with the historical and cultural ramifications of the long journey of black men through the Western nightmare and the recognition that, despite diversity, Blacks everywhere are an African people."

George, Felicia. "Black Woman, Black Man." *Harvard Journal of Afro-American Affairs*, 2 (1971), 1-17.

In *dem,* the story of white male America, Kelley also tells the story of Black America. Both worlds are dependent on each other.

Jařab, Josef. "The Drop of Patience of the American Negro." *Philologica Pragensia*, 12 (1969), 159-170.

Kelley's first two novels deal with a search for identity. His first novel, *A Different Drummer,* written in social, historical and political terms and in the form of a fantasy was "excellent." However, his second novel, *A Drop of Patience,* which dealt with the search in terms of culture can only be accepted with reservation. The "drop in patience which is characteristic of the social scene [in *A Drop of Patience*],...result[s] in a drop of artistic value and effectiveness."

"Kelley, William Melvin." *Black American Writers Past and Present: A Biographical and Bibliographical Dictionary.* Theressa Gunnels Rush, Carol Fairbanks Myers and Ester Spring Arata. Metuchen, New Jersey: The Scarecrow Press, Inc., 1975. II, 453-454.

Biographical data: birth, education, family professional experiences, awards, publications and address.

Klotman, Phyllis R. "An Examination of the Black Confidence Man in Two Black Novels: *The Man Who Cried I Am* and *dem.*" *American Literature,* 44 (January 1973), 596-611.

Calvin Coolidge Johnson, "Cooley," a character in Kelley's *dem* is a contemporary con man but is in the "trickster" tradition of Afro-American folklore, the one who brings "about a sense of solidarity in the black community."

—. "The Passive Resistant in *A Different Drummer, Day of Absence* and *Many Thousand Gone.*" *Studies in Black*

Literature, 3 (Autumn 1972), 7-11.

The Running Man is one of the Black writer's metaphors. William Melvin Kelley in *A Different Drummer* shows the running of Tucker Caliban as a positive act of renunciation, the action of a self-reliant man. Running is an escape, an act of passive resistance.

—. "The White Bitch Archetype in Contemporary Black Fiction." *Bulletin of the Midwest Modern Language Association,* 6 (Spring 1973), 96-110.

Tam in *dem* falls from her pedestal as white goddess and serves as "the instrument of...[the Black man's] revenge against [sic] the total, oppressive society."

Nadeau, Robert L. "Black Jesus: A Study of Kelley's *A Different Drummer.*" *Studies in Black Literature,* 2 (Summer 1971), 13-15.

He makes extensive use of the transcendental concept of self-reliance. This concept is most evident in Tucker Caliban's African ancestor who is not docile and submissive but a redeemer of his people—he is the Black Jesus. Kelley suggests that the Black man will achieve personal freedom when he relies upon his own intuitive moral sense.

Schraufnagel, Noel. *From Apology to Protest: The Black American Novel.* Deland, Florida: Everett/Edwards, Inc., 1973, pp. 174-177.

A Different Drummer is a militant protest novel with a non-violent revolution.

Singh, Raman K. "The Black Novel and Its Tradition." *Colorado Quarterly,* 20 (Summer 1971), 23-29.

A Different Drummer portrays the Identity-Quest as a discovery of identity rather than a loss of identity.

Starke, Catherine Juanita. *Black Portraiture in American*

Fiction: Stock Characters, Archetypes, and Individuals. New York: Basic Books, Inc., 1971, pp. 120-123, 154-155, 228-230.

Kelley utilizes the archetypal patterns of sacrifice symbol or victim of cultural and environmental determinism in *A Drop of Patience,* and the primitive, *dem.* In terms of the Black individual, he uses the Black avenger, *A Different Drummer.*

Weyl, Donald M. "The Vision of Man in the Novels of William Melvin Kelley." *Critique,* 15 (Number 3), 15-33.

Kelley's early novels show an optimistic vision of Black and white relationship; however, by 1967, he seems to see no "road to re-integration for man."

Whitlow, Roger. *Black American Literature: A Critical Study.* Chicago: Nelson Hall, 1973, pp. 158-161.

Biographical data and a discussion of his first novel, *A Different Drummer* and his satire *dem.*

"William Melvin Kelley." *Dark Symphony: Negro Literature in America.* Edited by James A. Emanuel and Theodore L. Gross. New York: Free Press, 1968, pp. 454-455.

Biographical and critical statement and a brief discussion of "Cry for Me."

D. *A Drop of Patience*

Bates, Arthenia J. Review of *A Drop of Patience* by William Melvin Kelley. *CLA Journal,* 9 (September 1965), 99-100.

The controlling metaphor of the book is blindness which chronicles a man's quest which becomes "the serach of a whole people" and which requires the careful reading "of a Henry James novel of *The Ambassadors'* era."

Boroff, David. "Ludlow Made His Own Music." *The New York Times Book Review,* 2 May 1965, pp. 40-41.

"A typical Negro novel...straight, unembellished naturalism" but it "is a moving, painful and stinging experience."

dem

Bates, Arthenia J. Review of *dem* by William Melvin Kelley. *CLA Journal,* 11 (June 1968), 374-376.

Kelley's third novel has as its "predominant theme...the decay of empire."

Bone, Robert. "Outsiders." *The New York Times Book Review,* 24 September 1967, pp. 5, 36, 38.

This satire in corrosive style and surreal grotesqueries is like the work of Nathanael West. Kelley is "bitter, disillusioned, alienated to the point of secession from American society."

Resnik, Henry S. "Nightmare of Today." *Saturday Review,* 28 October 1967, p. 40.

This is "a formless novel" which is an angry portrait of American society and "takes a good hard crack at our slim hold on reality."

Dunsfords Travels Everywhere

Smith, Cynthia. "New Departures in Prose." *Freedomways,* 11 (1971), 205-206.

This novel shows Kelley's experiment with style and form. The weakness of the novel is not the technique, but the confusion of meaning.

ARNOLD KEMP (1938—)

A. Arnold Kemp was born in Miami, Florida, in 1938. His family moved to Harlem when he was in the fourth grade. He has been a busboy, dishwasher, messenger and petty hustler. He spent a period in the Air Force. In 1959, he was jailed for robbery. While in prison, he seriously turned to writing and finished high school. When he was released in 1967, he entered Queens College under New York City's S.E.E.K. Program and graduated in 1970. He attended Harvard as a gradute student and now teaches English Literature at Medgar Evers College at the City University of New York.

B. Kemp, Arnold. *Eat Of Me, I Am the Savior.* New York: William Morrow and Company, Inc., 1972.

This is the story of Yaquii Lester who fires on the assassins of Nicholas Said, a popular Black Muslim leader, and kills two. As a result, he is jailed for seven years. When he is released, he pulls the Brotherhood together. However, three days after his release he is killed.

C. "Harlem to Harvard and Back." *Time,* 19 October 1970, p. 64.

Kemp talks about his life and the SEEK Program as his " 'instrument for making it.' "

"Kemp, Arnold." *Black American Writers Past and Present: A Biographical and Bibliographical Dictionary.* Theressa Gunnels Rush, Carol Fairbanks Myers, and Esther Spring

Arata. Metuchen, New Jersey: The Scarecrow Press, Inc., 1975. II, 455.

Lists all known works by Kemp.

D. *Eat Of Me, I Am the Savior*

Grant, Liz. Review of *Eat Of Me, I Am the Savior* by Arnold Kemp. *Black World*, 22 (November 1972), 90-91.

The book "slices through the messianic dream that Black people so tenaciously cling to and shows...a young hero to be, smack up against the realities of his time." The writing is good, but Yaquii Laster is one-dimensional.

JOHN OLIVER KILLENS (1916—)

A. John Oliver Killens was born in Macon, Georgia, on January 14, 1916. He has attended Edward Waters College, Morris Brown College, Atlanta University, New York University, the Law School of Howard University, Terrell Law School and Columbia University. He has taught and served as writer-in-residence at both Fisk University and Howard University.

B. Killens, John Oliver. *'Sippi.* New York: Trident Press, 1967.

This is the story of Charles "Chuck" Othello Chaney, his family and friends. It is also the tale of Carrie Louise Wakefield and her father James Richard Wakefield, the richest man in Wakefield who posed as a liberal friend of the Blacks. Charles and the other

Blacks defy those folk who would deny them of their manhood.

—. *The Cotillion: Or One Good Bull is Half the Herd.* New York: Trident Press, 1971.

This is a satirical novel about the conflicts between Black identity and white cultural image aspirations in the Black middle-class. The novel depicts the efforts of Daphne Lovejoy to coerce her daughter, Yoruba, into taking part in the Grand Cotillion. For Daphne believes the race will be "uplifted" by imitating whites. Yoruba's boy friend Ben Ali Lumumba, a self-appointed revolutionary, attempts to aid Yoruba and Daphne in an acceptance and awareness of their Black identity.

—. *A Man Ain't Nothin' But a Man.* Boston: Little, 1975.

The story recounts the life of John Henry, the Black steel-drivin' man, in the South during the period following slavery.

C. Bigsby, C. W. E. "From Protest to Paradox: The Black Writer at Mid Century." *The Fifties: Fiction, Poetry, Drama.* Edited by Warren French. Deland, Florida: Everett/Edwards, Inc., 1970, pp. 220-221.

Killens' first two books are rooted in the protest tradition, and in these he allows the cause to supercede art.

Gayle, Addison, Jr. *The Way of the World: The Black Novel in America.* Garden City, New York: Anchor Press/ Doubleday, 1975, pp. 261-277.

Killens "is the spiritual father of the novelists." He is the first of the modern period to have as his dominant theme the discovery of Black heritage, a Black awareness and the portrayal of proud Black men and women. His "characters are delineated by the extent of their love and faith in black people." The other achievement of Killens was "to opt for reality over illusion, no matter how devastating that reality."

Ihde, Horst. "Black Writer's Burden: Remarks on John Oliver Killens." *Zeitschrift für Anglistik und Amerikanistik,* 16 (January 1968), 117-137.

Killens has developed from the progressive author of *Youngblood* in which he demonstrates optimism and struggling humanism to the reactionary author *And Then We Heard the Thunder* in which he expresses the ideological concept of Black Nationalism.

Jackson, Blyden. "Killens, John Oliver." *Contemporary Novelists.* Edited by James Vinson. New York: St. Martin's, 1972, pp. 715-716.

Biographical data, publications listed and a discussion of his racial views as seen in his writing.

"Killens, John Oliver." *Black American Writers Past and Present: A Biographical and Bibliographical Dictionary.* Theressa Gunnels Rush, Carol Fairbanks Myers and Esther Spring Arata. Metuchen, New Jersey: The Scarecrow Press, 1975. II, 461-463.

Biographical data, criticism about Killens and his known published works are listed.

Killens, John Oliver. "The Black Writer Vis-á-Vis His Country." *The Black Aesthetic.* Edited by Addison Gayle, Jr. Garden City, New York: Anchor Books, 1972, pp. 357-373.

The American Negro must write about himself and in so doing he writes about America—its inhumanity, brutality and violence. Even though white America has tried to forget, deny and destroy its history, the Negro cannot, he "must face...[it] squarely in order to transcend it."

"Killens, John Oliver." *Living Black American Authors: A Biographical Directory.* Ann Allen Shockley and Sue P. Chandler. New York: Bowker, 1973, p. 89.

Biographical data: birth, education, family, professional experience, memberships, awards, publications and address.

Killens, John Oliver. "Rappin' with Myself." *Amistad 2.* Edited by John A. Williams and Charles F. Harris. New York: Vintage Books, 1971, pp. 97-136.

Killens discusses his relationship with the world, his views, his writing—Black influences: Langston Hughes, Margaret Walker and Richard Wright—his audience, and critics, the Black writer and Blackness in general.

Killens, John Oliver. "Reflections from a Black Notebook." *Black Creation,* 2 (April 1971), 12-14.

His themes have been that Blacks are essentially beautiful and humanistic, an affirmation of the inalienable, non-negotiable right of self defense and that African Americans have always been ready for America to be free. However, Killens' greatest difficulty as a writer is knowing where he is going but not how to get there.

Klotman, Phyllis R. "The White Bitch Archetype in Contemporary Black Fiction." *Bulletin of the Midwest Modern Language Association,* 6 (Spring 1973), 96-110.

Martha Mae Jefferson in Killens' *Youngblood* allows her men to " 'lynch and castrate Negroes' " in her name. She is "desexed and victimized by the 'rape consciousness' of others.

Mitchell, Loften. "Three Writers and a Dream." *Crisis,* 72 (April 1965), 219-223.

Brief discussion of Killens' play *Lower Than the Angels,* a section from his novel *Youngblood,* and his film career.

Schraufnagel, Noel. *From Apology to Protest: The Black American Novel.* Deland, Florida: Everett/Edwards, Inc., 1973, pp. 174, 178-179, 183-184.

Killens' *And Then We Heard the Thunder* and *'Sippi* show "the increasing impatience of blacks about the racial policies of the country.

Wiggins, William, Jr. "Black Folktales in the Novels of John O. Killens." *The Black Scholar,* 3 (November 1971), 50-58.

Killens utilizes folktales in *Youngblood* and *And Then We Heard the Thunder,* but they are not inextricably woven into the plots. However, in his third novel, *'Sippi,* he uses the structure and the theme of a Black folktale as the basic outline.

—. "The Structure and Dynamics of Folklore in the Novel Form: The Case of John O. Killens." *Keystone Folklore Quarterly,* 17 (1972), 92-118.

In *Youngblood, And Then We Heard the Thunder* and *'Sippi,* Killens uses the folktale for humor and a variation on the theme of Black manhood. However, in *'Sippi* there is a more judicious use of folktale. The novel and the folktale have the same structure, style and theme—"black social protest and an emerging black manhood."

D. *'Sippi*

Jones, John Henry. "Killens' Fine, Sensitive New Novel." *Freedomways,* 7 (1967), 373-375.

'Sippi is "a poetic tapestry, richly woven with folkways speech, movement, ideas, colors, smells, sounds and emotions.

Williams, Ronald. Review of *'Sippi* by John O. Killens. *Negro Digest,* 17 (November 1967), 85-86.

This is a "classically bad novel with plodding events which lead nowhere."

The Cotillion, or One Good Bull is Half the Herd

Bond, Jean Carey. "Killens' New Novel a Satire on Black 'Society.' " *Freedomways,* 11 (1971), 203-205.

> This is a bitter and "compassionate exploration of the fables of black bourgeois sassiety." It compares to Chester Himes' *Pinktoes* in theme; the latter is better.

Davis, George. Review of *The Cotillion* by John O. Killens. *Black World,* 20 (June 1971), 51-52.

> This book is a reflection of undemented Black love written in "Afro-Americanese" in the style of a "barbershop bullshitter."

Frakes, James R. Review of *The Cotillion* by John O. Killens. *The New York Times Book Review,* 17 January 1971, pp. 4, 34-35.

> This is not a novel in the traditional sense although it does have an action line, a climactic event, and conflict. The book is "like a caricature-missle" in which everything is triple life-size.

AUDREY LEE

A. Audrey Lee, a short story writer, poet and novelist, was born in Philadelphia. She attended the West Philadelphia High School and Temple University's Community College.

B. Lee, Audrey. *The Clarion People.* New York: McGraw-Hill Book Company, 1968.

The story of Lillian Peoples, a believer in God and a truster in humanity, spiritual agony and redemption. She moves from her rural home to the city in search of excitement. Here, she finds numerous wretched and lost souls and almost loses her own.

C. "First Novelists." *Library Journal,* 93 (February 1, 1968), 579.

Lee gives autobiographical data and a statement about her creation of *The Clarion People*.

WILLIAM MAHONEY (1941–)

A. William Mahoney was born October 1, 1941.

B. Mahoney, William. *Black Jacob.* New York: Macmillan, 1969.

The story is of Dr. Jacob Blue, a Black Mississippi physician, who decides to run for Congress. The story points out Blue's ambivalence between his bourgeois professional friends and his real constituency—the poor Blacks. He discovers too late that he has to think and accept his Blackness.

C. "Mahoney, William." *Black Writers Past and Present: A Biographical and Bibliographical Dictionary.* Theressa Gunnels Rush, Carol Fairbanks Myers, and Esther Spring Arata. Metuchen, New Jersey: The Scarecrow Press, Inc., 1975. II, 519.

Lists all of the known works of Mahoney.

D. *Black Jacob*

Bambara, Toni Cade.   Review of *Black Jacob* by William Mahoney. *Liberator,* 10 (May 1970), 20.

There are flaws in the book, but the author has chosen an involved task—"to give the complex web of...the magnolia society."

Karp, David.   Review of *Black Jacob* by William Mahoney. *The New York Times Book Review,* 9 March 1969, p. 38.

Mahoney is too close to his narrator. However, he does succeed "brilliantly in individual vignettes depicting the harrowing daily occurrences which the Southern black accepts as part of his unique lifestyle."

CLARENCE MAJOR (1936–)

A. Clarence Major was born in Atlanta, Georgia, on December 31, 1936. He has studied at The Art Institute in Chicago, Armed Forces Institute and the University of Wisconsin. He has worked as an essayist, short story writer, poet, novelist, research analyst, editor, instructor and anthologist.

B. Major, Clarence. *All-Night Visitors.* New York: Olympia, 1969.

Eli Bolton's odyssey to a foster home in Chicago, the Vietnam War, a return to Chicago and Roosevelt College and to New York's

Lower East Side is recounted. The result of this odyssey is a proclamation by him that he is "firmly a man." This comes at the end of the book.

Major, Clarence. *No.* New York: Emerson Hall Publishers, Inc., 1973.

Moses Westby is losing his wife. He is incapable of satisfying her sexually. The story centers on Westby's childhood experiences, those which rendered him incapable of satisfying her. There is in this novel a shifting pattern of reality.

C. "Clarence Major." *Interviews with Black Writers.* Edited by John O'Brien. New York: Liveright, 1973, pp. 125-139.

Major's concern is with experimentation in the form of the novel and the definition of the "I." He sees imagination and real life as inseparable and language more than "actual experience, time and place." Reality is ever changing, not fixed. He discusses his novels.

"Major, Clarence." *Black American Writers Past and Present: A Biographical Dictionary.* Theressa Gunnels Rush, Carol Fairbanks Myers and Esther Spring Arata. Metuchen, New Jersey: The Scarecrow Press, 1975. II, 520-524.

The listing includes biographical data, criticism of Major and a list of his known published works.

"Major, Clarence." *Contemporary Authors.* Edited by Barbara Harte and Carolyn Riley. Detroit, Michigan: Gale Research Company, 1970. XXIII-XXIV, 274-275.

Biographical data: personal, career, writings, work in progress and biographical/critical sources.

Major, Clarence. *The Dark and the Feeling: Black American Writers and Their Works.* New York: The Third Press,

115

1974, pp. 115-153.

Major discusses his novels (*All-Night Visitors* and *No*), writing, criticism, critics (Black and white), Black literature, aesthetics, publishing and censorship.

—. "Making Up Reality: Clarence Major on New Fiction and Criticism." *Fiction International*, 2/3 (1974), 151-154.

Fiction of the 70's "will rediscover content or 'dynamic situations' in static or new terms" as a result of its response to the novels of the 60's which for the most part were "killjoys" and "static."

Shepperd, Walt. "An Interview with Clarence Major and Victor Hernandez Cruz." *New Black Voices: An Anthology of Contemporary Afro-American Literature.* Edited by Abraham Chapman. New York: Mentor Books, 1972, pp. 545-552.

Discusses Black writing, aesthetics, *All-Night Visitors*, publishing, racism and the novel form.

This interview also appears in *Nickel Review*, 12 September 1969 and *Dark and Feeling* by Clarence Major.

D. *All-Night Visitors*

Lehmann-Haupt, Christopher. "Books of the Times: On Erotica." *The New York Times*, 7 April 1969, p. 41.

"The trouble with his novel is that the arrangement of the material doesn't build or sustain anything but boredom."

Miller, Adam David. Review of *All-Night Visitors* by Clarence Major. *Black Scholar*, 2 (January 1971), 54-56.

The book is more than an exploitation of sex, it is a view of the life of our modern cities through the eyes of Eli Bolton, a sensitive observer.

No

Davis, George. Review of *No* by Clarence Major. *The New York Times Book Review*, 1 July 1973, p. 22.

> This is a book "readers are unlikely to set aside the time to dig for the rewards in this almost encoded work." Its strength is "in the shocking images" and it "proves that European Protestants are not the only men on earth pursued by Calvinistic demons."

Walker, Jim. Review of *No* by Clarence Major. *Black Creation*, 4 (Summer 1973), 44-45.

> The novel treats the theme of imprisonment, self-awareness, personal liberation and violence. "Major writes excellently well, even if we don't always agree with or totally understand what he is saying."

PAULE MARSHALL (1929—)

A. Paule Marshall, novelist and short story writer, was born in Brooklyn, New York, on April 9, 1929. She graduated Phi Beta Kappa from Brooklyn College in 1953. She has worked as a librarian in New York and as a journalist for the magazine *Our World*. She has received awards from the Guggenheim and Ford Foundation, the National Institute of Arts and Letters, the National Endowment for the Arts, and the Yaddo Corporation.

B. Marshall, Paule. *The Chosen Place, the Timeless People.*

New York: Harcourt, 1969.

Saul Amron, a Jewish-American anthropologist, his wife and a research associate go to Bournehills on a multimillion-dollar development scheme for a United States foundation. Amron plans to conduct an anthropological study of the West Indian island and then develop the community. However, this community of acne-cutters and fisherfolk clings to its heritage and resists all efforts to modernize it.

C. Braithwaite, Edward. "Rehabilitations." *The Critical Quarterly,* 13 (September 1971), 175-183.

> *The Chosen Place, the Timeless People* has as its point "that we are creatures of our history, that the past predicts our present and that the present is, in the end, what we call 'home.' "

"West Indian History and Society in the Art of Paule Marshall's Novel." *Journal of Black Studies,* 1 (December 1970), 225-238.

> Paule Marshall suggests in *The Chosen Place, The Timeless People* that "the hard ground for development lies...in the discovery of one's self in the life and history of one's people."

Brown, Lloyd W. "The Rhythms of Power in Paule Marshall's Fiction." *Novel,* 7 (Winter 1974), 159-167.

> Marshall's novels combine ethnic and feminist themes with an emphasis on power. Her interest in power-physical force, willpower, political and sexual power—is shown in the cyclical structure of her works and the use of rhythms like that of machines or calypso dances.

Giddings, Paula. "A Special Vision, a Common Goal." *Encore American and Worldwide News,* 23 June 1975, pp. 44-48.

> "Paule Marshall consistently uses the theme of cultural conflict to

activate her characters."

Kapai, Leela. "Dominant Themes and Technique in Paule Marshall's Fiction." *CLA Journal,* 16 (September 1972), 49-59.

Her major themes are quest for identity, the race problem, the importance of tradition for the Black American and the need for sharing to achieve meaningful relationships. Her plots are unambiguous but interesting; she uses symbolism and frequently focuses on the subconscious mind of the characters. She excels in her character portrayal, but she is at her best in her portrayal of Black women.

"Marshall, Paule." *Black American Writers Past and Present: A Biographical and Bibliographical Dictionary.* Theressa Gunnels Rush, Carol Fairbanks Myers and Esther Spring Arata. Metuchen, New Jersey: The Scarecrow Press, Inc., 1975. II, 527-528.

Lists all her known works and some articles of criticism about her.

Marshall, Paule. "Reading." *Mademoiselle,* 79 (June 1974), 82-83.

Marshall says Ralph Ellison's *Shadow and Act* is her "literary Bible" because it articulates clearly and precisely what she believes the Black Experience to be and the role and responsibility of the Balck writer.

—. "Shaping the World of My Art." *New Letters,* 40 (Autumn 1973), 97-112.

Marshall discusses her early influences, the role of Black literature, her major themes—"the importance of truly confronting the past, in both personal and historical terms, and the necessity of reversing the present order"—and her works.

Miller, Adam David. Review of *Brown Girl, Brownstones* by Paule Marshall. *The Black Scholar,* 3 (May 1972), 56-58.

This is a story about Selina Boyce's rites of passage, her family and the Brooklyn Brownstones that house them. "There is a very nicely kept balance between psychological, cultural and social causes, which gives depth and vividness to characterization and a rightness to action."

Nazareth, Peter. "Paule Marshall's Timeless People." *New Letters,* 40 (Autumn 1973), 113-131.

"The Chosen Place, The Timeless People is a Third-world novel with...[a] message to all the exploited peoples of the world." The message is that the whole system must change, one cannot forget his roots, and that exploited peoples alienate themselves, not merge. The problem in the Third World is that history has not changed, the people are still being exploited.

"Paule Marshall." *Dark Symphony: Negro Literature in America.* Edited by James A. Emanuel and Theodore L. Gross. New York: Free Press, 1968, 400-401.

Biographical data, a critical statement and a brief discussion of "Brazil."

Reilly, John M. "Marshall, Paule." *Contemporary Novelists.* Edited by James Vinson. New York: St. Martin's, 1972, 849-850.

Biographical data, a list of her publications, and a discussion of her novels—*The Chosen Place, The Timeless People* and *Brown Girl, Brownstones.*

Schraufnagel, Noel. *From Apology to Protest: The Black American Novel.* Deland, Florida: Everett/Edwards, Inc., 1973, pp. 137-139.

Marshall in *The Chosen Place, The Timeless People* "illustrates the tendency of an oppressed people to establish a racial identity in which they can take pride."

Skeeter, Sharyn J. "Black Women Writers: Levels of Identity." *Essence*, 4 (May 1973), 58-59, 76, 89.

Marshall describes male-female relationships in other than violent terms.

Starke, Catherine Juanita. *Black Portraiture in American Fiction: Stock Characters, Archetypes and Individuals.* New York: Basic Books, Inc., 1971, pp. 241-243.

The Chosen Place, The Timeless People depicts the Black individual in a "day-to-day interaction with other blacks, with some whites, and in situations forcing them to take critical looks at their lives."

Stoelting, Winifred L. "Time Past and Time Present: The Search for Viable Links in *The Chosen Place, The Timeless People* by Paule Marshall." *CLA Journal*, 16 (September 1972), 60-71.

Marshall's search for " 'viable links' " shows that man's survival in the future is dependent upon a knowledge of a brutal past.

Washington, Mary Helen. "Black Women Image Makers." *Black World,* 23 (August 1974), 10-18.

Marshall has established images that are so powerful they can "combat whatever stereotypes of Black women still persist."

Whitlow, Roger. *Black American Literature: A Critical History.* Chicago: Nelson Hall, 1973, pp. 139-141.

Biographical data and a statement about *Brown Girl, Brownstones*—the "story of the youth and maturation of Selina Boyce."

D. *The Chosen Place, The Timeless People*

Bond, Jean Carey. "Allegorical Novel by Talented Storyteller." *Freedomways*, 10 (1970), 76-78.

The book has a sound structure, but "Mrs. Marshall strikes her symbolic chords with too heavy a hand, as if she feared we might miss the point." The best parts of the novel are "the dialogues in West Indian dialect."

SHARON BELL MATHIS (1937–)

A. Sharon Bell Mathis, novelist and teacher, was born in Atlantic City, New Jersey, on February 26, 1937. She attended Morgan State College. She has received an award from the Council on Interracial Books for Children, American Library Association, and the Coretta Scott King Award. She writes a monthly column for *Ebony Jr.* magazine and is writer-in-residence at Howard University.

B. Mathis, Sharon Bell. *Sidewalk Story.* New York: Viking, 1970.

The story of Lilly Etta Allen who is appalled that her mother and the neighbors do nothing when Lilly's best friend's family, a mother and seven children, is evicted. She fights to publicize the deed and help her friend in this plight.

—. *Teacup Full of Roses.* New York: Viking, 1972.

The story covers one week in the life of a Black family. There are three boys—Joe, David and Paul. Paul, the oldest and favored, is a drug addict. Because of the favoritism shown Paul, Joe and Davey's life is made miserable. The story is experienced through Joe who is to graduate from night school during the week the story takes place. Joe finally realizes he must forego his own dreams because of his mother's devotion to Paul and his brilliant younger brother's need for family guidance and support.

—. *Listen for the Fig Tree.* New York: Viking, 1974.

The story of a sixteen-year-old Black blind girl's attempt to get her mother through the first Christmas after the death of her father and her desire to go to her first Kwanza.

—. *The Hundred Penny Box.* New York: Viking, 1975.

This is the story of Michael and his great, great aunt, Dewbet Thomas. When she comes to live with his family, he and his aunt become co-conspirators against his mother who is uneasy with Aunt Dew in the house. Michael and his aunt like it best when she goes through her memories with the aid of her one-hundred-penny-box, a box which holds a penny for every year of her life.

C. Parks, Carole A. "Goodbye Black Sambo: Black Writers Forge New Images in Children's Literature." *Ebony,* 28 (November 1972), 60-70.

Mathis, who "writes for black youths coping with ghetto adolescence," explains her feelings about Black children and Black fiction.

"Mathis, Sharon Bell." *Black American Writers Past and Present: A Biographical and Bibliographical Dictionary.* Theressa Gunnels Rush, Carol Fairbanks Myers and Esther Spring Arata. Metuchen, New Jersey: The Scarecrow Press, Inc., 1975. II, 535-536.

Biographical data and a list of "all known published books."

"Mathis, Sharon Bell." *Living Black American Authors: A Biographical Directory.* Ann Allen Shockley and Sue P. Chandler. New York: Bowker, 1973, p. 107.

Biographical data: personal, sidelights, career, writings, photograph, work in progress and a source of additional information.

"Writers and Writings." *Negro History Bulletin,* 38 (April/

May 1975), 380-381.

Biographical data and a brief summary of each of her books to date.

D. *Teacup Full of Roses*

Cortez, Rochell. "Books for the Young." *Black Books Bulletin,* 1 (Summer/Fall 1973), 35.

It "drags at times" but the problem presented is a universal one.

Greenfield, Eloise. Review of *A Teacup Full of Roses* by Sharon Bell Mathis. *Black World,* 22 (August 1973), 86-87.

This is "a story of sacrifice, of the kind of love that has enabled Black brothers and sisters to survive even when their parents have become physically or emotionally exhausted from the grueling conditions under which we live." This is "a book to grow on."

The Hundred Penny Box

Gottlieb, Annie. Review of *The Hundred Penny Box* by Sharon Bell Mathis. *The New York Times Book Review,* 4 May 1975, pp. 20-21.

It depicts a universal experience and "makes you think of whoever has been old and dear in your life." It talks incidentally of old age and death; it does not preach.

Louise M. Meriwether

LOUISE M. MERIWETHER

A. Louise Meriwether was born in Haverstraw, New York. She attended New York University and the University of California at Los Angeles. She has been a reporter for the *Los Angeles Sentinel,* a story analyst at Universal Studios and a staff member of the Watts Writer's Workshop. Her work has appeared in *Antioch Review, Negro Digest, Frontier* (now merged with *The Nation*) and *Sepia.*

B. Meriwether, Louise. *Daddy Was a Number Runner.* Englewood Cliffs, New Jersey: Prentice-Hall, 1970.

> The story of twelve-year-old Francie Coffin, the daughter of a number runner, growing up in Harlem in the 1930's. She has to face the desertion of her father, the jailing of her brother on murder charges and the dropping out of school of her other brother.

C. "Involved." *Black World,* 22 (January 1973), 90.

> Report of Meriwether's efforts to protect the Black image.

Meriwether, Louise. *"Daddy Was a Number Runner." Ebony,* 25 (July 1970), 98-103.

> Excerpts from the novel, comments by James Baldwin taken from the book's forword, illustrations, and a brief biography.

"Meriwether, Louise M." *Black American Writers Past and Present: A Biographical and Bibliographical Dictionary.*

Theressa Gunnels Rush, Carol Fairbanks Myers and Esther Spring Arata. Metuchen, New Jersey: The Scarecrow Press, Inc., 1975.

Biographical data and a list of "all known published books."

"Meriwether, Louise M." *Living Black American Authors: A Biographical Directory.* Ann Allen Shockley and Sue P. Chandler. New York: Bowker, 1973, p. 110.

Biographical data: birth, education, professional experience, memberships, publications and address.

D. *Daddy Was a Number Runner*

Clarke, John Henrik. "Honest Novel About Harlem." *Freedomways*, 10 (1970), 381-382.

This is a healthy, hopeful and sad, but honest novel.

Giovanni, Nikki. Review of *Daddy Was a Number Runner* by Louise Meriwether. *Black World*, 19 (July 1970), 85-86.

This book gives a positive picture of the Black experience, tells of a "Black girl who is a Black woman," and causes the reader to share Francie's experiences.

King, Helen. Reivew of *Daddy Was a Number Runner* by Louis Meriwether. *Black World*, 19 (May 1970), 51-52.

The novel takes place in Harlem in the 1930's "but the tale is timeless for millions of...people who take their joy in their dreams when the real is no longer bearable."

TONI MORRISON (1931—)

A. Toni Morrison was born in Lorain, Ohio, on February 18, 1931. She attended Howard University and Cornell University. She is a former teacher and is at present an editor at Random House.

B. Morrison, Toni. *The Bluest Eye.* New York: Holt, 1970.

> This is the story of Pecola Breedlove as told by Claudia MacTeer. They are both growing up in Ohio of the 1940's. Pecola is poor, Black and pregnant by her drunken father. She has seen her mother focus her attention on blue eyed Polly, the little girl she takes care of; as a result she, Pecola, wants blue eyes. But she does not want every day blue eyes, but The Bluest Eye—so blue everyone will notice and be in awe of her.

—. *Sula.* New York: Alfred A. Knopf, 1973.

> This is the story of the friendship of two Black women—Nel and Sula—in The Bottom of Medallion, a small town in Ohio. They meet in 1922, when they are twelve and share everything up until Nel marries. Sula then leaves town and is gone for ten years. When they meet again, they realize things have changed, and Nel no longer understands Sula.

C. "Conversations with Alice Childress and Toni Morrison/The Co-Editors." *Black Creation Annual* (1974-75), pp. 90-92.

Toni Morrison discusses criticism and major themes and ideas in

Black writing today.

"Morrison, Toni." *Black American Writers Past and Present: A Biographical and Bibliographical Dictionary.* Theressa Gunnels Rush, Carol Fairbanks Myers and Esther Spring Arata. Metuchen, New Jersey: The Scarecrow Press, Inc., 1975. II, 55-556.

Lists works by Morrison, book reviews and a brief biographical sketch.

"Morrison, Toni." *Contemporary Authors.* Edited by Clare D. Kinsman and Mary Ann Tennenhouse. Detroit, Michigan: Gale Research Company, 1972. XXIX-XXXII, 429.

Biographical data: personal, career, writings, work in progress and biographical/critical sources.

Parks, Carole A. "Goodbye Black Sambo: Black Writers Forge New Images in Children's Literature." *Ebony,* 28 (November 1972), 60-70.

Morrison "attempts...to establish various relationships between the Dick-and-Jane fantasies of childhood and the damage later caused to black adults."

D. *The Bluest Eye*

Dee, Ruby. "Black Family Search for Identity." *Freedomways,* 11 (1971), 319-320.

Toni Morrison "gives us a sense of some of the social elements of some of the people, black and white, that contribute to the erosion of innocence and beauty."

Grant, Liz. Review of *The Bluest Eye* by Toni Morrison. *Black World,* 20 (May 1971), 51-52.

This novel explores the theme of self hatred, a theme which has probably not been treated since Ralph Ellison's young invisible man.

Loftin, Elouise. Review of *The Bluest Eye* by Toni Morrison. *Black Creation,* 3 (Fall 1971), 48.

An "experience/book" which will make the reader "want to bite, scratch, kick, scream and kill and in the end create something beautiful."

Sissman, L. E. "Beginner's Luck." *The New Yorker,* 23 January 1971, pp. 92-94.

This is "one of the most painful and acute studies of black childhood...ever read."

Sokolov, Raymond A. Review of *The Bluest Eye* by Toni Morrison. *Newsweek,* 30 November 1970, pp. 95-96.

The tone of "this lyrical story...is of Black conversation." Morrison "has found a way to express...[political] consciousness in a novel instead of a harangue."

Wilder, Charles M. "Novels by Two Friends." *CLA Journal,* 15 (December 1971), 253-255.

A book which demonstrates its author's "optimism" and its strongest point is its "superb dialogue." The main character, Pecola Breedlove, "is a universal figure."

Sula

Blackburn, Sara. Review of *Sula* by Toni Morrison. *The New York Times Book Review,* 30 December 1973, p. 3.

"The setting and the characters continually convince and intrigue, the novel seems somehow frozen, stylized."

Jefferson, Margo. "Toni Morrison: Passionate and Precise." *Ms.,* 3 (December 1974), 34-38.

Review of *Sula* and tangentially *The Bluest Eye;* both books are "confident...filled with pleasure and pain and what Virginia Woolf calls 'that curious sexual quality which comes only when sex is unconscious of itself.' The language is passionate and precise; lyrical and philosophical."

McClain, Ruth Rambo. Review of *Sula* by Toni Morrison. *Black World,* 23 (June 1974), 51-53.

Sula is a "thought provoking story" and is full of "sophisticated symbols...[and] numerous images of three."

O'Connor, Douglas. Review of *Sula* by Toni Morrison. *Black Creation Annual,* 6 (1974-1975), 65-66.

"Ms. Morrison has written a novel about the shape of love. She has told us of its futility, of its pain." Her themes are Black women and Black love.

Smith, Barbara. "Beautiful Needed Mysterious." *Freedomways,* 14 (1974), 69-72.

No one has written of the Black experience like Morrison since Zora Neale Hurston and Jean Toomer. "As significant as her rootedness in Black life, is the fact that her perspective is undeniably feminine."

WILLARD MOTLEY (1912-1965)

A. Willard Motley was born in Chicago, Illinois, on July 14, 1912. His literary career began in 1922 with the introduction of a column called "Bud Billiken" in the *Chicago Daily Defender.* He is best known for his novel *Knock on Any*

Door (1947) and as such became one of the major writers of the forties. His last novel was published posthumously in 1966. He died of gangrene in Mexico City, March 4, 1965.

B. Motley, Willard. *Let Noon Be Fair.* New York: Putnam's, 1966.

> Las Casas, a Mexican fishing village, is a virtual Eden. The natives live their lives uninhibited. However, gradually Americans inundate the village—tourists, residents, greedy businessmen. The village becomes as the villagers had feared, a resort town—a decadent tourist trap.

C. Bigsby, C. W. E. "From Protest to Paradox: The Black Writer at Mid Century." *The Fifties: Fiction, Poetry, Drama.* Edited by Warren French. Deland, Florida: Everett/Edwards, Inc., 1970, 221-222.

> Motley is rooted in the protest tradition and is unabashedly naturalistic.

Bayliss, John F. "Nick Romano: Father and Son." *Negro American Literature Forum,* 3 (Spring 1969), 18-21.

> Review of the naturalistic novels *Knock on Any Door* in which Nick Romano appears and *Let No Man Write My Epitaph* in which the son of Nick Romano appears.

Giles, James R. "The Short Fiction of Willard Motley." *Negro American Literature Forum,* 9 (Spring 1975), 3-10.

> Motley's short stories are important because some of them are good and because they work out themes—Black and Chicano identity, women's consciousness, and homosexuality—which he later used in his published works.

—. "Willard Motley's Concept of 'Style' and 'Material':

Some Comments Based Upon the Motley Collection at the University of Wisconsin." *Studies in Black Literature*, 4 (Spring 1973), 4-6.

Motley believed any detail could be used as long as it "was appropriate to the 'envionment' of the work." This idea of freedom sheds "some light on the 'apparent' formlessness of his art."

— and Jerome Klinkowitz. "The Emergence of Willard Motley in Black American Literature." *Negro American Literature Forum*, 6 (Summer 1972), 31-34.

Motley's writing career began in 1922, but he was not recognized until 1947 with the publication of *Knock on Any Door.*

Klinkowitz, Jerome, James Gile and John T. O'Brien. "The Willard Motley Papers at the University of Wisconsin." *Resources for American Literary Study*, 2 (Autumn 1972), 218-169.

Lists the "letters, correspondence, documents, memorabilia, manuscripts and working notes" of Willard Motley "housed in the Rare Book Room of the University of Wisconsin Memorial Library" and gives a brief biographical sketch.

"Motley, Willard." *Black American Writers Past and Present: A Biographical and Bibliographical Directory.* Theressa Gunnels Rush, Carol Fairbanks Myers and Esther Spring Arata. Metuchen, New Jersey: The Scarecrow Press, Inc., 1975. II, 557-558.

Lists critical articles, works by Motley and a brief biography of him.

Rayson, Ann L. "Prototypes for Nick Romano of *Knock on Any Door:* From the Diaries in the Collected Manuscripts of the Willard Motley Estate." *Negro American Literature Forum*, 8 (Fall 1974), 248-251.

By reading Motley's twenty-nine diaries, one can see the growth of an artist and his creations. Nick Romano of *Knock on Any Door* is based on an actual person, Joe Nuaves of Denver, Colorado. Using the material in his diary, he wrote a short story, "The Boy," and from this short story, he later wrote the novel, *Knock on Any Door.*

"Willard Motley Dies in Mexico; Author of '*Knock on Any Door.*' " *The New York Times,* 5 March 1965, p. 30.

Obituary.

Major, Clarence. "Willard Motley: Vague Ghost After the Father." *The Dark and Feeling: Black American Writers and Their Works.* New York: The Third Press, 1974, pp. 95-97.

Describes an "uncomfortable" meeting with Motley and gives some background information on Motley.

Woods, Charles. "The *Adventure* Manuscript, New Light on Willard Motley's Naturalism." *Negro American Literature Forum,* 6 (Summer 1972), 35-38.

Adventures is an "autobiographical narration of two journeys from Chicago to the West Coast taken by Motley between late November of 1936 and the summer of 1938" which covers 474 typewritten pages. It demonstrates an affirmaion of the beauty and significance of the lowest strata of humanity.

D. *Let Noon Be Fair*

Byrd, James W. "Story of Man's Innate Selfishness and Greed." *Phylon,* 27 (Fall 1966), 306-308.

This novel is not as good as *Knock on Any Door.* The point is sometimes confusing and the satire outweighs the humor.

Donoso, Jose. "From Heaven to Hilton." *Saturday Review,* 12 March 1966, p. 152.

This is "a story...so linear and so relentless in its tracking of decay ...that it leaves no place for irony."

Randall, Dudley. Review of *Let Noon Be Fair* by Willard Motley. *Negro Digest,* 15 (May 1966), 90-91.

This is a novel about whites seen through "the objective ironical eye of a Negro." The style is panoramic and the reader is involved.

ALBERT MURRAY (1916—)

A. Albert Murray was born in Nokomis, Alabama, in 1916. He grew up in Mobile and was educated at Tuskegee and later taught there. In addition to Tuskegee Institute, he attended New York University. He has been O'Connor Professor of Literature at Colgate University, Visiting Professor of Literature at the University of Massachusetts (Boston) and Paul Anthony Brick lecturer at the University of Missouri. His previously published non-fiction books include *The Omni-Americans, South to a Very Old Place* and *The Hero and the Blues.* His essays, criticism and short stories have appeared in various periodicals.

B. Murray, Albert. *Train Whistle Guitar.* New York: McGraw-Hill, 1974.

This is a novel about a twelve-year-old boy, Scooter, growing up in Gasoline Point, Alabama, in the 1920's. He and his friend, Buddy Marshall, want to be like their friend, Luzana Charley, the steel blue twelve-string guitar player, roust-about and world traveler.

C. "Albert Murray." *Dark Symphony: Negro Literature in America.* Edited by James A. Emanuel and Theodore L. Gross. New York: Free Press, 1968, pp. 374-375.

Biographical and critical statement and a brief discussion of "Train Whistle Guitar," the short story.

Beauford, Fred. "A Conversation with Al Murray." *Black Creation,* 3 (Summer 1972), 26-27.

Murray discusses his book *South to a Very Old Place,* "the new folklore of white supremacy," and the nature of art and politics.

"Murray, Albert." *Black American Writers Past and Present: A Biographical and Bibliographical Dictionary.* Theressa Gunnels Rush, Carol Fairbanks Myers and Esther Spring Arata. Metuchen, New Jersey: The Scarecrow Press, Inc., 1975. II, 561-562.

Biographical data, photograph and works by and about the author are given.

"Murray, Albert." *Contemporary Authors.* Edited by Clare D. Kinsman. Detroit, Michigan: Gale Research Company, 1975. XLIX-LII, 393.

Biographical data: personal, career, writings, work in progress, sidelights and avocational interests.

Sheppard, R. Z. "Soul: Straight Up, No Ice." *Time,* 10 January 1972, p. 65.

Review article of *South to a Very Old Place* but includes data about the author.

D. *Train Whistle Guitar*

Edwards, Thomas R. "Can You Go Home Again?" *New York Review of Books,* 13 June 1974, pp. 38-39.

The book sentimentalizes the past but is alive and interesting.

Hudson, Theodore R. Review of *Train Whistle Guitar* by Albert Murray. *The Black Scholar,* 7 (September 1975), 51-52.

"Murray explores facets of the Southern-ness of black people in a well wrought, warm, and good-humored story." There is no "heavy social or political significance in...[the] novel."

Mercier, Vivian. "Gasoline Ain't Blues." *Saturday Review/ World,* 4 May 1974, p. 51.

"The most abiding impression left by this book...is not its content but its form." There is in this book a "joy in language for its own sake."

ROBERT DEANE PHARR (1916—)

A. Robert Deane Pharr was born in Richmond, Virginia, on July 5, 1916. He attended St. Paul's College, Lincoln University, Virginia Union University and Fisk University. He has had one of his novels made into a movie.

B. Pharr, Robert Deane. *The Book of Numbers.* Garden City, New Jersey: Doubleday, 1969.

Dave Green, the twenty-two year old hero of the novel, arrives in town Easter 1935 with a large bankroll and a dream to start banking numbers. Three years after having a number of adventures and joining with Blueboy Harris, his gambling operation has grown and prospered, making him one of the richest Negroes in the world.

Pharr, Robert Deane. *S.R.O.* Garden City, New York:
Doubleday, 1971.

> Sid Bailey checks into the Logan Hotel in Harlem after a three-week
> drunk. In this single room occupancy hotel, he begins to write a
> book. The writing of the book is his escape from wine and a way
> of discovering a past and a future. Here at the SRO are explored
> welfare hotels, life in the ghettos created by narcotics, aberrant
> sex, wine, poverty and other aspects of existence on "public
> assistance."

—. *The Soul Murder Case.* New York: Avon/Equinox Books,
1975.

> Bobby Dee, a Black entertainer, who has become a literary agent
> describes his life and hard times. This includes his relationship
> with a legendary blues singer.

C. Land, Irene Stokvis, editor. "First Novelists." *Library Journal,* 96 (October 1, 1968), 3591.

> Pharr talks of his life and his purpose in writing *The Book of
> Numbers.*

O'Brien, John and Raman K. Singh. "Interview with Robert
Deane Pharr." *Negro American Literature Forum,* 8 (Fall
1974), 244-246.

> Pharr discusses *The Book of Numbers, S.R.O.,* his writing schedule
> and his beliefs about writing—a man writes because he has to and
> no "novel will have a real social impact."

"Pharr, Robert D(eane)." *Contemporary Authors.* Edited
by Clare D. Kinsman. Detroit, Michigan: Gale Research
Company, 1975. XLIX-LII, 426.

> Biographical data: personal, career, writings, work in progress and
> sidelights.

Whitlow, Roger. *Black American Literature: A Critical History.* Chicago: Nelson Hall, 1973, pp. 165-167.

> Brief biographical statement and a discussion of *The Book of Numbers.* It is "the best novel of black urban 'sporting life' in black American literature—it surpasses McKay's famous *Home to Harlem.*" Both its subject and design are distinctive.

C. *The Book of Numbers*

Hairston, Loyle. "Enjoyable Novel with Weak Theme." *Freedomways,* 10 (1970), 384-386.

> It has flaws but is "an impressive novel which is peopled with such a lively assortment of characters that the reader is guaranteed some enjoyable reading."

"Taken for Granite." *Time,* 6 June 1969, pp. 113-115.

> The moral of the book is that "crime may sometimes pay, but being black never does."

CARLENE HATCHER POLITE (1932—)

A. Carlene Hatcher Polite was born August 28, 1932, in Detroit. She attended Sarah Lawrence and studied dance under Martha Graham. She has been a dancer and pursued various other careers, including guest instructor at Wayne State University.

B. Polite, Carlene Hatcher. *The Flagellants.* New York: Farrar,

1967.

> This is the story of Ideal and Jimson who are in New York. They meet, fall in love and live in Greenwich Village. They later part. However, while they are together, they flagellate each other by tearing off "layer after layer of rationalization and myth."

C. Gross, Robert A. "The Black Novelists: 'Our Time.' " *Newsweek,* 16 June 1969, pp. 94-98.

> Carlene Hatcher Polite has a bleak outlook in *The Flagellants,* though she says her aim in writing is the " 'transformation of people' " even though she has doubts about the novel as a medium.

Lottmann, Herbert R. "Authors and Editors." *Publishers' Weekly,* 12 June 1967, pp. 20-21.

> Biographical data and a statement concerning *The Flagellants,* " 'The theater of Cruelty' in book form."

"Polite, Carlene Hatcher." *Contemporary Authors.* Edited by Barbara Harte and Carolyn Riley. Detroit, Michigan: Gale Research Company, 1970. XXIII-XXIV, 334.

> Biographical data: career, writings, work in progress, sidelights and biographical/critical sources.

Schraufnagel, Noel. *From Apology to Protest: The Black American Novel.* Deland, Florida: Everett/Edwards, Inc., 1973, pp. 129-130.

> *The Flagellants* "illustrates that Negroes must maintain their self-respect and make a special effort to adjust themselves to a society in which the males tend to be emasculated and the females tend to emerge as the dominant force."

D. *The Flagellants*

Ebert, Roger. "First Novels by Young Negroes." *The American Scholar,* 36 (Autumn 1967), 682, 686.

This is a book which makes one wish the author had not told so truthfully of a hopeless human agony.

Raphael, Frederic. "Jimson and Ideal." *The New York Times,* 11 June 1967, p. 40.

There is an uncertainty in expression and in intention on the part of the author.

Sayre, Nora. "Punishing." *The Nation,* 9 October 1967, p. 344.

The Flagellants is more essay than novel, but worthwhile and not bound into a racial tradition.

ISHMAEL REED (1938–)

A. Ishmael Reed was born in Chattanooga, Tennessee, on February 22, 1938. He attended the State University of New York at Buffalo. He is a writer and lecturer.

B. Reed, Ishmael. *The Free-Lance Pallbearers.* Garden City, New York: Doubleday, 1967.

This is the story of Bukka Doopeyduk in a kingdom called HARRY SAM. Here, the inhabitants are obsessed with excrement and the society is full of violence and passive hypocrisy.

Reed, Ishmael. *Yellow Back Radio Broke-Down.* Garden City, New York: Doubleday, 1969.

> This is a Western in which a lone cowboy, the Loop Garoo Kid, rescues the town of Yellow Back from the evil grip of Drag Gibson, the proverbial cattle baron. In the development of the novel, Reed satirizes the American Dream.

—. *Mumbo Jumbo.* Garden City, New York: Doubleday, 1972.

> This is a detective novel. The Black hoo-doo artists, jazz enthusiasts and spiritual descendants of the much maligned Osiris, are being opposed by the evil white Atonists, co-opters and bastardizers of the magic tradition.

—. *The Last Days of Louisiana Red.* New York: Random, 1974.

> This is the story of the Louisiana Red Corporation, a criminal mail-order house specializing in juke boxes, Black record companies and hard drugs. It was founded by a New Orleans witch whose guiding spirit was Minnie the Moocher, who lives off of the energy of her victims. The alternative to the Red Peril is Ed Yellins' Solid Gumbo Works. There is a conspiracy to eliminate Yellins' business and it is up to PaPa LaBas to work it out.

C. Abel, Robert H. "I Am a Cowboy in the Boat of Ra." *Explicator,* 30 (May 1972), Item 81.

> In this poem, Reed couples popular culture and Egyptian mythology to develop the idea that the Black "god Ra is about to reclaim his throne and his power over men" from his brother Set.

Ambler, Madge. "Ishmael Reed: Whose Radio Broke Down?" *Negro American Literature Forum,* 6 (Winter 1972), 125-131.

> Reed uses the themes he developed in "I Am a Cowboy in the Boat

of Ra" in *Yellow Back Radio Broke-Down*—hypocrisy of the American Church, Black woman's emasculation of the Black male, communist party, warping of history to confuse and degrade the Black man, image of the Black man as evil, open attempts of the white man to kill off the Black man. This is a novel which "spans the time gap from 1000 B.C. to the present."

Beauford, Fred.   "A Conversation with Ishmael Reed." *Black Creation,* 4 (Winter 1973), 12-15.

He discusses his motives for writing in his particular style, anti-Judeo-Christian values, an inclination for humor and the surprise element, Christianity and Hoo Doo, language and *The Yardbird Reader.* He sees himself as working in the Surrealist sense.

Cooper, Arthur.   "Call Him Ishmael." *Newsweek,* 2 June 1975, p. 70.

The Richard and Hinda Rosenthal Foundation Award for 1975 went to Ishmael Reed, the most controversial writer ever to receive the award, for his satirical novel *The Last Days of Louisiana Red.*

Duff, Gerald.   "Reed's *The Free-Lance Pallbearers.*" *Explicator,* 32 (May 1974), Item 69.

Reed parodies "Ellison's thematic and structural use of the grandfather's advice." His parody is "hilarious, but its implications are bleak."

Fenderson, Lewis H.   "The New Breed of Black Writers and Their Jaundiced View of Tradition." *CLA Journal,* 15 (September 1971), 18-24.

Reed believes that the absurdity of this country is reflected in the communications media and the best weapon the Black man has is satire.

Ford, Nick Aaron.   "A Note on Ishmael Reed: Revolutionary Novelist." *Studies in the Novel,* 3 (1971), 216-218.

Ishmael Reed

"The most revolutionary black novelist who has appeared in print thus far is Ishmael Reed." In his novels *The Free-Lance Pallbearers* and *Yellow Back Radio Broke-Down,* he makes a "comic-satirical assault on the Establishment." In one book his hero is a Black student dropout and in the other a Black cowboy.

Gayle, Addison, Jr. "Reed, Ishmael." *Contemporary Novelists.* Edited by James Vinson. New York: St. Martin's, 1972, pp. 1053-1054.

Biographical data, list of publications and a discussion of Reed as "our most important Black satirist."

Gross, Robert A. "The Black Novelists: 'Our Time.' " *Newsweek,* 16 June 1969, pp. 94-98.

Ishmael Reed calls for a Black aesthetic and in so doing breaks with the traditional novelistic device.

"Ishmael Reed." *Black American Literature: A Critical History.* Roger Whitlow. Chicago: Nelson Hall, 1973, pp. 154-157.

Biographical data, mentions briefly "I Am a Cowboy in the Boat of Ra" and *Yellow Back Radio Broke-Down,* and discusses the satire in *The Free-Lance Pallbearers.*

"Ishmael Reed." *Interviews with Black Writers.* Edited by John O'Brien. New York: Liveright, 1973, pp. 165-183.

His influences have been Nathanael West, popular culture and Vaudeville. He is seeking a reform of the imagination to render the soul of a person in the novel and to tell a story, not write a novel. He satirizes "emblems of the cultural establishment and its underlying values." He sees himself as a fetish maker. He discusses *The Free-Lance Pallbearers, Yellow Back Radio Broke-Down* and mentions *Mumbo Jumbo.*

This interview also appears in *Fiction International,* Summer 1973.

"Ishmael Reed." *The New Fiction: Interviews with Innovative American Writers.* Joe David Bellamy. Urbana: University of Illinois Press, 1974, pp. 130-141.

In an interview by John O'Brien, the collaboration of fiction and other fields of art as the direction for writing is stressed by Reed. He discusses *Mumbo Jumbo* and "D Hexorcism of Noxon D Awful," the artist as prophet, the use of factual and imaginative material, critics and his essay writing techniques.

Lewald, H. Ernest, editor. *The Cry of Home: Cultural Nationalism and the Modern Writer.* Knoxville: The University of Tennessee Press, 1972, pp. 235-238.

"The Afro-American novel reaches its highest achievement in Ishmael Reed." His *Free-Lance Pallbearers* "is a radical departure from the usual protest novel." It is "hysterically funny" but "unbearably honest."

Major, Clarence. "catechism of d neoamerican hoodoo church, Poems by Ishmael Reed." *The Dark and Feeling: Black American Writers and Their Works.* New York: The Third Press, 1974, pp. 53-54.

He lauds Reed's original style, awareness and use of historical and cultural background in his first collection of poetry.

—. "The Explosion of Black Poetry." *Essence,* 3 (June 1972), 44-47, 66.

Reed is a poet who goes "directly to the heart of Blackness" and believes he has been " 'buffaloed by many aspects of American society.' "

"Reed, Ishmael." *Black American Writers Past and Present: A Biographical and Bibliographical Dictionary.* Theressa Gunnels Rush, Carol Fairbanks Myers and Esther Spring Arata. Metuchen, New Jersey: The Scarecrow Press, Inc., 1975. II, 623-635.

Ishmael Reed

Biographical data, criticism about Reed and a list of his known published works are given.

Reed, Ishmael. "Can a Metronome Know the Thunder or Summon a God?" *The Black Aesthetic.* Edited by Addison Gayle, Jr. Garden City, New York: Anchor Books, 1972, pp. 381-382.

The New Literary Neo-Hoo Dooism finds artists exhibiting their own individualism and responding to their own spirits.

"Reed, Ishmael." *Contemporary Authors.* Edited by Barbara Harte and Carolyn Riley. Detroit, Michigan: Gale Research Company, 1970. XXIII-XXIV, 348.

Biographical data: personal, career, writings, work in progress, sidelights and biographical/critical sources.

"Reed, Ishmael." *Contemporary Literary Criticism.* Edited by Carolyn Riley and Barbara Harte. Detroit, Michigan: Gale Reserach Company, 1974. II, 367-369.

Critical statements on *Mumbo Jumbo* and *Conjure.*

Reed, Ishmael. "Introduction." *19 Necromancers from Now.* Edited by Ishmael Reed. Garden City, New York: Doubleday, 1970.

Black and white writers who fail to conform are ignored in America. The new Black writers show "a marked independence from Western form." These new writers represent a national scope and show along with the writings of Indian-Americans and Chinese-Americans that print and words are not dead. He discusses some of the new Afro-American writers.

This essay also apperas in *New Black Voices,* edited by Abraham Chapman (New York: Mentor Books, 1972).

—. "Ishmael Reed on Ishmael Reed." *Black World.* 23 (June 1974), 20-34.

145

He discusses his novels: *Mumbo Jumbo, Yellow Back Radio Broke-Down;* his views on Baldwin and Ellison; views on Black poetry; his present work: *The Last Days of Louisiana Red,* his autobiography and *The Yardbird Reader;* his most experimental work: "D Hexorcism of Noxon D Awful," and why he's "so mean and hard."

Schmitz, Neil. "Neo-HooDoo: The Experimental Fiction of Ishmael Reed." *Twentieth Century Literature,* 20 (April 1974), 126-140.

Reed's fiction particularly after *Free-Lance Pallbearers* is "denial of the 'dominant culture.' " In this denial, he has developed what he calls Neo-HooDoo which has moved him "along the same metafictive angle that Pynchon and Barthelme take." He is distinguished from them in his belief that print and words are still alive.

"When State Magicians Fail: An Interview with Ishmael Reed." *Nickel Review,* 1 (August 28, 1968), 4-6.

Reed discusses *The Free-Lance Pallbearers,* some Black writers and critics.

This interview also appears in Nick Aaron Ford's *Black Insights* and in the *Journal of Black Poetry,* Summer-Fall 1969.

D. *The Free-Lance Pallbearers*

Cade, Toni. Review of *The Free-Lance Pallbearers* by Ishmael Reed. *Liberator,* 9 (June 1969), 20.

This is a book which is written in the apocalyptic tradition of Ray Bradbury and Kurt Vonnegut. The great achievement of the book is its language and length.

Joyce, Barbara. "Satire and Alienation." *Phylon,* 29 (Winter 1968), 409-411.

In this satire, the picaresque character Bukka Doopeyduk is the "good" Negro. Reed utilizes features of the Gothic novel and attacks such topics as Blacks and whites, avant-garde and mass culture, politics and the University of Buffalo.

Kinnamon, Keneth. Review of *The Free-Lance Pallbearers* by Ishmael Reed. *Negro American Literature Forum,* 1 (Winter 1967), 18.

Reed is amused and outraged at the state of the nation but only finds outlet in this book for his amusement.

Tucker, Martin. Review of *The Free-Lance Pallbearers* by Ishmael Reed. *Commonweal,* 87 (January 26, 1968), 508.

He cannot "be called a camp follower, his novel inverts conventional attitudes for sustained comic effect; his feints are brilliant and his punches swift...he is prone to rely on the in-joke, and to... 'grotest' too much."

Woodford, John. Review of *The Free-Lance Pallbearers* by Ishmael Reed. *Negro Digest,* 18 (February 1969), 68-69.

Reed uses the imaginary country device of satire and "captures the...bathroom texture and odor of American life."

Yellow Back Radio Broke-Down

Bush, Roland E. "Werewolf of the Wild West (on a Novel by Ishmael Reed)." *Black World,* 23 (January 1974), 51-52.

"Reed combines the qualities of Afro-American dialect and slang and western jargon." As an anarchist and rebellious artist, he is trying to effect a "revolution of the mind."

Test, George A. "The Cliche as Archetype." *Satire Newsletter,* 7 (Fall 1969), 79-80.

Yellow Back Radio Broke-Down has "a folksy tone," contains "a richness of cliche that is mind blowing," and has "enmeshed...

[within it] at least three levels of comment."

Mumbo Jumbo

Baker, Houston A., Jr. Review of *Mumbo Jumbo* by Ishmael Reed. *Black World*, 22 (December 1972), 63-64.

This book "offers an entrancing ratiocinative tale, a conspiracy view of history, a critical handbook for the student of the Black Arts, and a guide for the contemporary Black consciousness intent on the discovery of its origins and meanings."

Bryant, Jerry H. "Who? Jes Grew? Like Topsy? No, Not Like Topsy." *The Nation*, 25 September 1972, pp. 245-247.

The tone is too serious, but Reed, the historical novelist, wins his reader over "by the breadth of his allusions and the seeming inexhaustibility of his imagination."

Edwards, Thomas R. "News from Elsewhere." *The New York Review of Books*, 5 October 1972, pp. 21-23.

"Reed opens fictional art to the forms and mythic possibilities of popular culture, pursuing not psychological description but a perspective on history."

Friedman, Alan. Review of *Mumbo Jumbo* by Ishmael Reed. *The New York Times Book Review*, 6 August 1972, 1, 22.

This book is "frankly and consummately freewheeling, part historical funferal, here a highbrow satire, here a low-key farce." It is written with black humor and its methods are not novelistic, it is original and a "cross between the craft of fiction and witchcraft."

Gordon, Andrew. "Spirits Abroad." *Saturday Review*, 14 October 1972, pp. 76-78.

Ishmael Reed

This is playful entertainment but also "a loving homage to the forgotten traditions of the Afro-American heritage."

Major, Clarence. Review of *Mumbo Jumbo* by Ishmael Reed. *Black Creation*, 4 (Fall 1972), 59-61.

This is Reed's masterpiece and like his other works is satirical. This word symphony "is concerned with the brash world of white assumptions about black people and culture in general."

Sheppard, R. Z. Review of *Mumbo Jumbo* by Ishmael Reed. *Time*, 14 August 1972, p. 67.

Reed is a welcome change from the club of LeRoi Jones, for he uses the feather, though this may be more deadly.

The Last Days of Louisiana Red

Baker, Houston A., Jr. Review of *The Last Days of Louisiana Red* by Ishmael Reed. *Black World*, 24 (June 1975), 51-52, 89.

This is not the book the others are; it is not well thought out, not truly original or as vivid. This does not negate the subject of his attack—"the radicals and run-aways of his own generation"—and that he is still "one of the finest writers around today."

Foote, Bud. "Reed Ladles Out a Rich, Hot Gumbo." *The National Observer*, 30 November 1974, p. 23.

The reader gets "not only a novel about business espionage, a detective story, a satire and a history of hoodoo, but a commentary on Greek tragedy and the role of the chorus therein."

Sheppard, R. Z. "Gumbo Diplomacy." *Time*, 21 October 1974, p. 11.

This book is "a combination circus freak show, detective story, Negro Dead Sea Scroll and improvised black-studies program" which will both amuse and offend Blacks.

149

BRYANT ROLLINS (1937—)

A. Bryant Rollins was born in Boston, Massachusetts, on December 13, 1937. He attended Northwestern University and the University of Massachusetts. He has worked as a reporter, editor, writer and lecturer. He is a novelist, poet and playwright.

B. Rollins, Bryant. *Danger Song.* New York: Doubleday, 1967.

> This is the story of a young Negro, Martin, who attempts to reach beyond his Boston ghetto. The story is set in the Roxbury section of Boston and concerns two families—one Negro and one white. Eventually, the Negro learns that he can only be what he is—an American Negro.

C. McQuade, Kate, editor. "First Novelists." *Library Journal,* 92 (February 1, 1967), 606-607.

> Rollins gives autobiographical and novelistic statements.

"Rollins, Bryant." *Black American Writers Past and Present: A Biographical and Bibliographical Dictionary.* Theressa Gunnels Rush, Carol Fairbanks Myers and Esther Spring Arata. Metuchen, New Jersey: The Scarecrow Press, Inc., 1975. II, 639-640.

> Biographical statement and a list of "all known published books."

"Rollins, Bryant." *Contemporary Authors.* Edited by Clare

D. Kinsman. Detroit, Michigan: Gale Research Company, 1975. XLIX-LII, 464-465.

Biographical data: personal, career, writings, work in progress and sidelights.

D. *Danger Song*

Hairston, Loyle. "Perceptive First Novel." *Freedomways,* 7 (1967), 265-267.

This is a "solid first novel" even though it has flaws.

McDonnell, Thomas P. "Promising Rookies." *The Critic,* 26 (August-September 1967), 72-75.

This novel is an "inside" glimpse of Roxbury, Boston's Harlem, for both "proper Bostonians and paddies." Here Rollins shows his "rich capacities for further creative effort."

GIL SCOTT-HERON (1949—)

A. Gil Scott-Heron was born in Chicago, Illinois, on April 1, 1949. He attended Fieldstone School of Ethical Culture, Lincoln University and Johns Hopkins University. He is a writer, vocalist and musician.

B. Scott-Heron, Gil. *The Vulture.* New York: World, 1971.

The novel is narrated by Spade, Junior Jones, Afro (Tommy Hall) and IQ (Ivan Quinn). The "vulture" is the deathrap of drugs and

151

drug traffic. The novel shows the vicious trap of men ensnared in the competitive dealing with drugs.

—. *The Nigger Factory.* New York: Dial, 1972.

The novel covers three days of a major crisis on the predominantly Black Sutton University campus in Virginia. The militants present the demands to the president who responds by closing down the university and trying to expel the culprits.

C. Earles, Horace. "Gil Scott-Heron: A Players Interview." *Players,* 2 (November 1975), 20-24, 42, 62-65.

Gil Scott-Heron discusses the need for education before organization and action to effect change, the responsibility of the Black media, The Midnight Band, the power of concerted effort and concentration, and the role of the artist—he is to make things understandable, not complicate them. It is important for us to know that " 'Nobody can do everything, but everybody can do something.' "

Ivy, Archie. " 'The Bottle'—First Hit in 5 Years." *Soul,* 12 May 1975, p. 10.

Scott-Heron turned to music to communicate positive images to and of Black people because " 'people aren't reading novels anymore.' " His single, "The Bottle," about the evils of alcohol in the ghetto became a hit.

Orth, Maureen. "Midnight News." *Newsweek,* 10 February 1975, p. 65.

Biographical data and his philosophy given. With his Midnight Band, he "wants to reach a young black audience...and to continue the African Oral tradition by speaking his poetry on records."

"Scott-Heron, Gil." *Black American Writers Past and Present: A Biographical and Bibliographical Dictionary.* Theressa Gunnels Rush, Carol Fairbanks Myers and

Esther Spring Arata. Metuchen, New Jersey: The Scarecrow Press, Inc., 1975. II, 656-657.

Biographical data and works by and about him are listed.

"Scott-Heron, Gil." *Contemporary Authors.* Edited by
Clare D. Kinsman. Detroit, Michigan: Gale Research
Company, 1974. XLV-XLVIII, 509.

Biographical data: personal, career, writings, work in progress
and sidelights.

D. *The Vulture*

Grant, Liz. Review of *The Vulture* by Gil Scott-Heron.
Black World, 20 (July 1971), 96-98.

The "point it seems...to make is that only illusions bring about dis-
illusionment." The book "stylistically...is innovative because it
doesn't harp on the autobiographical."

The Nigger Factory

Davis, L. J. Review of *The Nigger Factory* by Gil Scott-
Heron. *Book World,* 12 March 1972, p. 10.

This "is not the traumatic, idealistic spasm of a white college but a
matter of the most desperate concern to everyone involved, radicals, moderates and administrators alike." It is a "pretty good
book" by a "young man who bears watching."

CHUCK STONE (1924–)

A. Chuck Stone was born in St. Louis, Missouri, on July 21, 1924. He attended Wesleyan Connecticut University and the University of Chicago. He has been an Air Force navigator, correspondent, instructor, editor and writer. He has won the Journalist of the Year award presented by the Capital Press Club in Washington, D.C., and the Alpha Phi Alpha of Chicago Award of Merit for Journalism. In 1969, he was Politician-in-Residence at Morgan State College.

B. Stone, Chuck. *King Strut.* New York: Bobbs-Merrill, 1970.

> This is a novel of contemporary politics. Handsome, charming and brilliant Hiram Elliott Quinault, Jr. is a Black congressman from Chicago. He is like other Congressmen in believing in high living and trying to get government contracts for his district. Although his color and chairmanship make him more vulnerable to scandal than others, he is neither prudent nor cautious in his behavior.

C. "Stone, Chuck." *Black American Writers Past and Present: A Biographical and Bibliographical Dictionary.* Theressa Gunnels Rush, Carol Fairbanks Myers and Esther Spring Arata. Metuchen, New Jersey: The Scarecrow Press, Inc., 1975. II, 684-685.

> Biographical data and works by and about him are listed.

"Stone, Chuck." *Living Black American Authors: A Biographical Directory.* Ann Allen Shockley and Sue P.

Chandler. New York: Bowker, 1973, pp. 152-153.

Biographical data: birth, education, family, professional experience, memberships, awards, publications and address.

D. *King Strut*

Blackwell, Angela. Review of *King Strut* by Chuck Stone. *The Black Scholar,* 2 (February 1972), 58-59.

The book is a "believable" and "true" story of America's first black Congressman ("obviously based on Adam Clayton Powell"). "It is a naked portrayal of the low, immoral, back-scratching, self interested workings of the United States government."

HENRY VAN DYKE (1928—)

A. Henry Van Dyke was born in Allegan, Michigan, on October 3, 1928. He attended the University of Michigan. He has won the Jule and Avery Hopwood Award for fiction, the Guggenheim Award in Creative Writing and the American Academy of Arts and Letters Award.

B. Van Dyke, Henry. *Ladies of the Rachmaninoff Eyes.* New York: Farrar, 1965.

Presents a protrait of two elderly widows who have developed a kinship beyond the boundaries of class, wealth and race. Their friendship is characterized by bickering, fussing and expressions of affection. The story of this relationship between Etta Klein, a rich Jewish lady, and Harriet Gibbs, her Black servant-companion, is told by seventeen-year-old Oliver, the nephew of Harriet Gibbs, who acts as surrogate for Etta Klein's dead son.

—. *Blood of Strawberries*. New York: Farrar, 1968.

Oliver, the narrator, is in his twenties and tells the story of a strange summer on the streets of Manhattan, in the Chelsea Hotel, at the St. Mark's Playhouse on Second Avenue. The novel is centered around Max Rhode, octogenarian litterateur, and his lifelong enemy-friend Orson Valentine. Their rivalry involves everything, especially their friendships, real or imagined, with Gertrude Stein.

—. *Dead Piano*. New York: Farrar, 1971.

Three Black radical extortionists force their way into a respectable surburban Black home. The home they invade in upper-middle-class St. Albans, New York, houses Olga Blake, Mr. Blake, an impassive gynecologist husband, and her uppity, Bennigtonbound daughter.

C. Starke, Catherine Juanita. *Black Portraiture in American Fiction: Stock Characters, Archetypes and Individuals*. New York: Basic Books, Inc., 1971, pp. 134-137, 209-214.

Van Dyke uses the archetypal mammy pattern in his *Ladies of the Rachmaninoff Eyes* and the Black individual character type of the youthful male in search of self in *Blood of Strawberries*.

"Van Dyke, Henry." *Contemporary Authors*. Edited by Clare D. Kinsman. Detroit, Michigan: Gale Research Company, 1975. XLIX-LII, 560.

Biographical data: personal, career, writings, work in progress, sidelights and biographical/critical sources.

D. *Blood of Strawberries*

Freedman, Richard. "Lamb Among Lions." *Book World*, 19 January 1969, p. 12.

It is "a highly literate and vastly entertaining suspense comedy," which is "sheer pleasure" to read.

Hicks, Granville. "Literary Horizons." *Saturday Review,* 4 January 1969, p. 93.

It is "a farce spiced with melodrama and mystery."

Dead Piano

Loftin, Elouise. Review of *Dead Piano* by Henry Van Dyke. *Black Creation,* 3 (Winter 1972), 54-55.

This is "a dead book" which is "sort of a hodgepodge of hodge-podges set to Mozart and Freud."

Robinson, Fern. Review of *Dead Piano* by Henry Van Dyke. *Black World,* 21 (June 1972), 86-87.

This "is a simple, untangled, easy-to-get-through thriller."

MELVIN VAN PEEBLES (1932—)

A. Melvin Van Peebles was born in Chicago, Illinois, on August 21, 1932. He grew up in Phoenix, Illinois, and attended Thornton Township High School, West Virginia State College and Ohio Wesleyan. He has written novels, plays, movies and music.

B. Van Peebles, Melvin. *A Bear for the F.B.I.* New York: Trident Press, 1968.

This is the story of Edward who recounts his boyhood—his earliest memories of Sunday mornings, his leaving home to go to school and his graduation. In the telling of the story, the narrator reveals the formation of his attitudes.

C. Abeke. "Van Peebles on the Inside." *Essence,* 4 (June 1973), 36-37, 62, 75.

An interview with Van Peebles which emphasizes the different Black points of view.

Bauerle, R. F. "The Theme of Absurdity in Melvin Van Peebles' *A Bear for the FBI." Notes on Contemporary Literature,* 1 (September 1971), 11-12.

The title of the novel and the explanatory note introduce "the reader to an absurd world...[which] claims to be real and honest but is actually full of fantasy and falsehood."

Coleman, Horace W., Jr. "Melvin Van Peebles." *Journal of Popular Culture,* 5 (Fall 1971), 368-384.

An interview in which Peebles discusses Blackness, art and his film, *Sweet Sweetback's Baadassss Song.*

Collier, Eugenia. "A Drama Review: *Aint Supposed to Die a Natural Death." Black World,* 21 (April 1972), 79-81.

Van Peebles has produced "a shallow treatment of profound trouble" and in so doing panders to the white opinion. The Black artist "must never present Black people as cute-talking clowns or helpless victims."

Gross, Robert A. "The Black Novelists: 'Our Turn.' " *Newsweek,* 16 June 1969, pp. 94-98.

Melvin Van Peebles says white publishers are only interested in works by Black writers if they lacerate or apologize to whites.

Gussow, Mel. "The Baadasssss Success of Melvin Van Peebles." *The New York Times Magazine,* 20 August 1972, pp. 14-15, 86-91.

He discusses Van Peebles and his art. Van Peebles' philosophy of life is "lynch me—if you can."

Lee, Don. "The Bittersweet of Sweetback/Or Shake Yo Money Maker." *Black World,* 21 (November 1971), 43-48.

"Sweet Sweetback's Baadasssss Song is a limited money-making, autobiographical fantasy of the odyssey of one Melvin Van Peebles through what he considered to be the Black community."

Schraufnagel, Noel. *From Apology to Protest: The Black American Novel.* Deland, Florida: Everett/Edwards, Inc., 1973, p. 126.

A Bear for the FBI emphasizes resignation and "illustrates the emptiness of life in a society that values conformity."

Scobie, W. I. "Supernigger Strikes." *London Magazine,* 12 (April/May 1972), 111-116.

Peebles' *Sweet Sweetback's Baadasssss Song* and others like it have caused a long-suffering stereotype of the Black's participation on and off screen to die.

"The Story of a 'Three-Day Pass.' " *Ebony,* 23 (September 1968), 54-56, 58-60.

Discussion of this film which Van Peebles wrote, scored, edited and directed.

"Van Peebles, Melvin." *Black American Writers Past and Present: A Biographical and Bibliographical Dictionary.* Theressa Gunnels Rush, Carol Fairbanks Myers, and Esther Spring Arata. Metuchen, New Jersey: The Scarecrow Press, Inc., 1975. II, 723-724.

Biographical data and a listing of the writers known works.

"Van Peebles, Melvin." *Contemporary Literary Criticism.* Edited by Carolyn Riley and Barbara Harte. Detroit, Michigan: Gale Reserach Company, 1974. II, 447-448.

> Critical statements on *Ain't Supposed to Die a Natural Death, Sweet Sweetback's Baadassss Song* and *Don't Play Us Cheap.*

Wolf, William. "B**da****s Peebles." *Milwaukee Journal Magazine,* 17 (September 1972), 33-35.

> Discussion of the life and career of Van Peebles.

MARY ELIZABETH VROMAN (1923-1967)

A. Mary Elizabeth Vroman was born in Brooklyn, New York, in 1923 and died in 1967. She was reared in the West Indies and attended Alabama State College. Her first story, "See How They Run," was filmed by Metro-Goldwyn-Mayer. She was the first Black woman to be a member of the Screen Writers' Guild.

B. Vroman, Mary Elizabeth. *Harlem Summer.* New York: Putnam's, 1967.

> Sixteen-year-old John Brown goes to Harlem from rural Alabama for a summer visit with his aunt and uncle. The conditions of the rural South are contrasted with those of the North as John in a new environment endeavors to find who he is.

C. Bachner, Saul. "Black Literature: The Junior Novel in the Classroom—*Harlem Summer.*" *Negro American Literature Forum,* 7 (Spring 1973), 26-27, 31.

> *Harlem Summer* is an "excellent means of exploring the black experience. It is thoroughly readable and explores all the issues."

"Mary Elizabeth Vroman, 42, A Writer and a Teacher Dies." *The New York Times,* 30 April 1967, p. 86.

> Obituary.

"Vroman, Mary Elizabeth." *Black Writers Past and Present: A Biographical and Bibliographical Dictionary.* Theressa Gunnels Rush, Carol Fairbanks Myers and Esther Spring Arata. Metuchen, New Jersey: The Scarecrow Press, Inc., 1975. II, 725-726.

> Biographical data, her known works and sources of criticism concerning her are listed.

ALICE WALKER (1944—)

A. Alice Walker was born in Eatonton, Georgia, on February 9, 1944. She attended Spelman College and Sarah Lawrence College. She has worked as a teacher and lecturer. She has won the American Scholar essay contest, the Merrill Fellowship for Writing and the National Endowment for the Arts Grant. She is a poet, novelist and essayist.

B. Walker, Alice. *The Third Life of Grange Copeland.* New York: Harcourt, 1970.

161

A novel about three generations of Black people, their struggle to overcome white oppression and their realization that there is Black oppression to overcome. Life in each generation represents a new locale and period in the life of Grange Copeland. In the first life, Grange Copeland is a heavy-drinking sharecropper living in the deep South. His second life begins when he flees the South to New York and returns to Georgia to begin his third life. Here, he realizes there is no excuse to desert one's human responsibilities.

C. "Alice Walker." *Interviews with Black Writers.* Edited by John O'Brien. New York: Liveright, 1973, pp. 185-211.

Walker's influences are Russian writers, Japanese haiku poets, Li Po, Emily Dickinson, e. e. cummings, Robert Graves, Ovid, Catullus, William Carlos Williams, Flannery O'Connor and Jean Toomer. She is concerned with the past and the possibility of change, Black people and woman—her oppressions, loyalties, insanities, triumphs and relationships. She discusses both her novel and her poetry.

"Alice Walker Talks About Black Women." *Encore,* 2 (April 1973), 41.

"Black women have more trouble in love" than anyone else and this is due to their perverted loyalty. At the same time she says, "I get very angry with Black women for taking all the stuff they take...they are the only people that I respect collectively and with no reservations."

Fowler, Carolyn. Review of *In Love and Trouble* by Alice Walker. *Freedomways,* 14 (1974), 59-62.

These stories portray "the authentic Heart of a Woman...the poignant, sad and unfulfilled heart."

Matteson, Robert. Review of *In Love and Trouble* by Alice Walker. *Fiction International,* 2/3 (1974).

The structure of many of her stories—"begin in the present, flashback to add psychological depth, then return to a present tense conclusion"—reinforces one of her "major themes...pressures of the past."

"Walker, Alice." *Black Writers Past and Present: A Biographical and Bibliographical Dictionary.* Theressa Gunnels Rush, Carol Fairbanks Myers and Esther Spring Arata. Metuchen, New Jersey: The Scarecrow Press, Inc., 1975. II, 727-729.

Biographical data, criticism on Walker and her known published works are given.

"Walker, Alice." *Contemporary Authors.* Edited by Clare D. Kinsman and Mary Ann Tennenhouse. Detroit, Michigan: Gale Research Company, 1973. XXXCII-XL, 524.

Biographical data: personal, career, writings, work in progress, sidelights and biographical/critical sources.

Washington, Mary Helen. "Black Women Image Makers." *Black World,* 23 (August 1974), 10-18.

Alice Walker has established images that are so powerful they can "combat whatever stereotypes of Black women still persist."

D. *The Third Life of Grange Copeland*

Coles, Robert. Review of *The Third Life of Grange Copeland* by Alice Walker. *New Yorker,* 27 February 1971, pp. 104-106.

This is not a social or protest novel, but a story, the story of a man who gains calm through an acceptance of his own worth. In this novel "the centuries of black life in America are virtually engraved on one's consciousness."

Cornish, Sam. Review of *The Third Life of Grange Copeland* by Alice Walker. *Essence,* 1 (April 1971), 20.

"Miss Walker pictures a family slowly broken under the white man's world, and the blackness we have to face one way or another ...It tells us what the non-fiction books could not, because of their polemical attitudes and structural forms."

Plumpp, Flavia D. Review of *The Third Life of Grange Copeland* by Alice Walker. *Black Books Bulletin,* 1 (Fall 1971), 26-27.

The novel "could be classified as philosophical or authoritative but definitely not entertaining." Miss Walker demonstrates the "ability to instill hope, instead of hopelessness and to build fire out of cold ashes,...an achievement not too often seen where novels are concerned."

Schorer, Mark. "Novels and Nothingness." *The American Scholar,* 40 (Winter 1970-1971), 168-174.

Walker "is not a finished novelist. She has much to learn. Fortunately, what she has to learn are the unimportant lessons, that is those that *can* be learned."

Shapiro, Paula Meinetz. "Pygmalion Reversed." *The New Leader,* 54 (January 25, 1971), 19-20.

A "compelling novel that emphasizes the humanity we share rather than the horrors of dehumanizing experiences."

MARGARET WALKER (1915—)

A. Margaret Walker, poet, novelist and teacher, was born in Birmingham, Alabama, on July 7, 1915. She attended Northwestern University and the University of Iowa. She has received the Rosenwald Fellowship for Creative Writing and the Houghton Mifflin Literary Award.

B. Walker, Margaret. *Jubilee.* Boston: Houghton, 1966.

> This is the story of Vyry, daughter of a plantation owner and his favorite slave, during the Civil War and Reconstruction. It tells of the endurance of this Black woman who was physically mistreated as a slave and harrassed by the Ku Klux Klan.

C. Emanuel, James A. "Walker, Margaret (Abigail)." *Contemporary Novelists.* Edited by James Vinson. New York: St. Martin's, 1972, pp. 1294-1296.

> Biographical data, list of her publications and a discussion of *Jubilee.*

Giddings, Paula. " 'A Shoulder Hunched Against a Sharp Concern': Some Themes in the Poetry of Margaret Walker." *Black World,* 21 (December 1972), 20-15.

> Walker's stress is upon Black folk history, a sense of roots, and the cyclical nature of reality and destiny.

—. "A Special Vision, a Common Goal." *Encore American and Worldwide News,* 23 June 1975, pp. 44-48.

> Margaret Walker explores themes of Civil War, Civil Rights Movement and the essence of Black people's lives in her novel and her poetry.

"Margaret Walker." *American Black Women in the Arts and Social Sciences: A Bibliographic Survey.* Ora Williams. Metuchen, New Jersey: The Scarecrow Press, Inc., 1973, pp. 87-88.

> List of Walker's works and some critical material.

165

"Margaret A. Walker." *Dark Symphony: Negro Literature in America.* Edited by James A. Emanuel and Theodore L. Gross. New York: Free Press, 1968, pp. 493-494.

Biographical data and a critical statement.

"Margaret Walker." *From the Dark Tower: Afro-American Writers 1900 to 1960.* Arthur P. Davis. Washington, D.C.: Howard University Press, 1974, pp. 180-185, 276.

She "is a better poet than...novelist" and explores the themes of the South, militance and brotherhood over and over. Her novel has too much of the "research that went into its making." A list of her published works and reference to some secondary material is included.

A Poetic Equation: Conversation Between Nikki Giovanni and Margaret Walker. Washington, D.C.: Howard University Press, 1974.

These two Black female poets discuss Vietnam, racial struggle and its future, new roles of the sexes, their philosophy of literature, their attitudes toward violence and compare the 60's with the 30's and 40's.

Rowell, Charles H. "An Interview with Margaret Walker." *Black World,* 25 (December 1975), 4-17.

Margaret Walker discusses her influences, the folk tradition in her poetry, *Jubilee,* William Styron's *Confessions of Nat Turner,* Langston Hughes, Richard Wright, Black Humanism, the Black Arts Movement and the Writer's Project of the WPA.

Schraufnagel, Noel. *From Apology to Protest: The Black American Novel.* Deland, Florida: Everett/Edwards, Inc., 1973, pp. 131-132.

Walker's *Jubilee* "emphasizes the ability of Negroes to survive in the face of great tribulations."

"Walker, Margaret." *Crowell's Handbook of Contemporary Poetry.* Edited by Karl Malkoff. New York: T. Crowell, 1973, pp. 319-322.

Brief biography, selected bibliography and a discussion of her two collections of poetry, *For My People* and *Prophets for a New Day.* In both books her verse represents her "deeply rooted sense of community" and the need for it to aggressively "assert its fundamental dignity."

Walker, Margaret. *How I Wrote Jubilee.* Chicago: Third World Press, 1972.

Walker discusses the creative process behind *Jubilee*—the idea, the research, and her influences. She also includes questions for discussion and a list of source materials used.

"Walker, Margaret S." *Living Black American Authors: A Biographical Directory.* Ann Allen Shockley and Sue P. Chandler. New York: Bowker, 1973, p. 164.

Biographical data: birth, education, family, professional experience, memberships, awards, publications and address.

"Walker, Margaret (Mrs. F. J. Alexander)." *Black American Writers Past and Present: A Biographical and Bibliographical Dictionary.* Metuchen, New Jersey: The Scarecrow Press, 1975. II, pp. 731-734.

Biographical sketch, list of her published works and a selected list of critical material.

Whitlow, Roger. *Black American Literature: A Critical History.* Chicago: Nelson Hall, 1973, pp. 136-139.

Biographical data and a discussion of her poetry and her novel, *Jubilee.* The novel "serves especially well as a response to white 'nostalgia' fiction about the antebellum and Reconstruction South." *Jubilee* is contrasted with *Gone with the Wind,* the latter being a poorer but more popular work.

D. *Jubilee*

Chapman, Abraham. "Negro Folksong." *Saturday Review,* 24 September 1966, pp. 43-44.

"In its evocation of the folk experience and folk attitudes of Southern Negroes on the plantation when slavery seemed to be a permanent institution, during the Civil War and the Reconstruction years, this...novel adds something different to the Civil War novel."

Davis, Lester. "The Passing of an Era." *Freedomways,* 7 (1967), 258-260.

Jubilee, an "epic, historical, and thoroughly researched novel, presents a different picture of an enslaved people from that of *Gone with the Wind. Jubilee* condemns bigotry, intolerance and slavery; it recognizes the need for Blacks and whites to unify.

"Southern." *Times Literary Supplement,* 29 June 1967, p. 583.

"There is a deep feeling for the beauty of the land" and "like the best Westerns, *Jubilee* adds something to the new American pastoral tradition."

JOHN EDGAR WIDEMAN (1941—)

A. John E. Wideman was born in Washington, D.C., on June 14, 1941. He attended the University of Pennsylvania and New College, Oxford. He has won the Kent Fellowship for Creative Writing from the University of Iowa, the Thouron Fellowship for Creative Writing, and he was a Ben Franklin Scholar and a Rhodes Scholar.

B. Wideman, John Edgar. *A Glance Away.* New York: Harcourt, 1967.

The two central characters are Eddie Lawson, a young Negro who has just returned to the South from an institution for drug addicts, and Robert Thurley, a middle-aged white professor of Comparative Literature at the local college, who is ridden by his homosexuality, alcoholism and memories of a domineering mother and unhappy marriage. These two meet through the intervention of Brother, the albino friend of Eddie. The story covers one day in the life of these men's lives and through a series of flashbacks, Eddie's previous life is revealed. There is a contest of wills between Eddie and Robert for Brother's friendship.

—. *Hurry Home.* New York: Harcourt, 1970.

This novel is written in the stream-of-consciousness style. It is the story of Cecil Braithwaite, a highly educated Black, who has earned a law degree and returned to his original occupation as house janitor. The main portion of the novel is concerned with his experiences while abroad after he left his wife in Europe, Africa and Spain.

—. *The Lynchers.* New York: Harcourt, 1973.

The novel focuses on four Black men in Philadelphia—Tom Wilkerson, Saunders, Rice and the dwarf Littleman. They are going to execute Littleman's plan to murder a Black whore, pin the murder on the white cop who is her secret pimp and then lynch the cop in front of the inflamed crowd. This plan is based on the assumption that things will never be the same after the killing.

C. Frazier, Kermit. "The Novels of John Wideman." *Black World,* 24 (June 1975), 18-38.

Wideman's three novels "develop through a weave of realistic and experimental elements: his major concerns—the significance of history which is unescapable in our lives and the ever-presence of a working imagination."

"John Wideman." *Interviews with Black Writers.* Edited by John O'Brien. New York: Liveright, 1973, pp. 213-223.

> He was influenced by Eliot, Defoe, Fielding, Sterne, Ellison, Wright, slave narratives and folklore. His unifying theme is an exploration of the imagination. In both *A Glance Away* and *Hurry Home,* he is interested in the formal aspects of the novel. He examines cultural collapse in *Hurry Home* and *The Lynchers.*

Shalit, Gene. "The Astonishing John Wideman." *Look,* 21 May 1963, pp. 31-36.

> Story and picture of John Wideman—formerly a Rhodes Scholar, playwright, poet, Phi Beta Kappa, novelist, formerly a basketball player and a teacher.

"Wideman, John E." *Black American Writers Past and Present: A Biographical and Bibliographical Dictionary.* Theressa Gunnels Rush, Carol Fairbanks Myers and Esther Spring Arata. Metuchen, New Jersey: The Scarecrow Press, Inc., 1975. II, 766-767.

> Biographical data is given, critical articles are cited, and all of his known publications are listed.

"Wideman, John E." *Living Black American Authors.* Ann Allen Shockley and Sue P. Chandler. New York: Bowker, 1973, p. 170.

> Biographical data: birth, education, family, professional experience, memberships, awards, publications and address.

D. *A Glance Away*

Caldwell, Stephen F. "Back Home in the Wasteland." *Saturday Review,* 21 October 1967, pp. 36-37.

> This is a book which moves the reader because of the author's artistry, not because of the plot.

Ebert, Roger. "First Novels by Young Negroes." *The American Scholar*, 36 (Autumn 1967), 682-686.

It has the plot of a good novel but employs stylistic tricks which mar the quality of the book.

Roskolenko, Harry. "Junkie's Homecoming." *The New York Times Book Review*, 10 September 1967, p. 56.

The author has managed to develop enormous objectivity in his characterization.

The Lynchers

Hairston, Loyle. "Exceptional Fiction by Two Black Writers." *Freedomways*, 13 (1973), 337-340.

"The Lynchers...demonstrates how intensely American the black writer is intellectually and spiritually." The style is unconventional, but effective. The novel is marred by a narrow vision and *righteous* tone. This is more a novel of language than of action.

Hudson, Jo. Review of *The Lynchers* by John E. Wideman. *Black Books Bulletin*, 2 (Spring 1974), 47-48.

A book which is not easy to read, utilizes a variety of techniques, and has little action but offers a great deal for reflection in race relations.

Prescott, Peter S. "Enough Rope." *Newsweek*, 7 May 1973, pp. 99-100.

It is vicious, a novel which is "forever getting under way and forever being distracted by brilliant digressions."

Walker, Jim. Review of *The Lynchers* by John E. Wideman. *Black Creation*, 5 (Fall 1973), 42-43.

This is an important book which is an intimate journey into the psyches of men intent on committing a revolutionary, ritualistic act. The author has a gift with words.

JOHN ALFRED WILLIAMS (1925—)

A. John A. Williams was born in Jackson, Mississippi, on December 5, 1925. He attended Syracuse University. He has worked as a public relations director, editor and publisher, announcer, correspondent, lecturer and interviewer. He won the Roman Fellowship of the American Academy of Arts and Letters Award; however, the award was rescinded by officials in Rome.

B. Williams, John A. *The Man Who Cried I Am.* Boston: Little, 1967.

> This is the story of Max Reddick, a Black expatriate writer, and his struggle to define himself outside of the white man's labels and his institution of racism. He is in Amsterdam struggling with his Blackness and dying of cancer. During this struggle, he discovers some secret information concerning the "King Alfred" plot, a plan of the American government to eliminate minority groups.

—. *Sons of Darkness, Sons of Light: A Novel of Some Probability.* Boston: Little, 1969.

> Sargeant Carrigan, Detective First Grade, shoots a Black youth five times in the chest and kills him. Eugene Browning, a Black man, of the Institute for Racial Justice conceives the idea of revenge by making a "Business Arrangement" with an old Mafia friend to have the cop murdered. However, the Mafia Don hires an Israeli gunman to do the "job." Meanwhile, Black militants have plans of their own.

172

—. *Captain Blackman: A Novel.* Garden City, New York: Doubleday, 1972.

> Captain Abraham Blackman is badly wounded in Vietnam. As he is recovering and suffering from delirium, there are flashbacks which allow Williams to explore the Black man's role in each consecutive war in American history. This includes the Revolutionary War, the War of 1812, the Civil War, the Indian wars, the Spanish-American War, World War I, the Spanish Civil War, World War II, the Korean War and Vietnam.

—. *Mothersill and the Foxes.* Garden City, New York: Doubleday, 1975.

> Odell Mothersill grows up during the depression, gets his degree in the 40's and becomes a Black case worker in the welfare institution in the 50's. He is concerned about people and part of this concern is for the "foxes," especially. As he searches for a meaningful love relationship, he becomes sexually involved with many foxes.

C. Beauford, Fred. "John A. Williams: Agent Provocateur." *Black Creation*, 2 (Summer 1971), 4-6.

> This is an interview in which Williams discusses conspiracies and his book, *The King God Didn't Save*, its purpose and reception.

Bryant, Jerry H. "John A. Williams: The Political Use of the Novel." *Critique: Studies in Modern Fiction*, 16, Number 3 (1975), 81-100.

> Williams' growth in his art and his political expression can be traced from his second novel, *Night Song*, to his more recent one, *The Man Who Cried I Am.* Believing that good art serves politics best, he tries through his art to present an accurate picture of society. In this picture, he tries to warn whites and encourage Blacks. He fuses pessimism and optimism and recognizes limitations. Thus, he presents a more human and realistic picture to politics and helps the reader avoid an oversimplification of the struggle. There is a clear definition of hero and villain.

Burke, William M. "The Resistance of John A. Williams: *The Man Who Cried I Am.*" *Critique: Studies in Modern Fiction,* 15, Number 3 (1974), 5-14.

"The theme of the novel seems to be that by resisting the oppressive forces of cancer and politics Max Reddick insists on the value and dignity of his life as a man and as a Black man and, by extension, affirms the value of all individual life." This has been Williams' concern in all his previous novels: "the need to affirm one's worth by resisting the racism that would deny it."

Cash, Earl A. "The Evolution of a Black Writer: John A. Williams." Ph.D. dissertation, University of New Mexico, 1972.

The study of Williams presents "an overview of Williams as a writer...an investigation of the author's metamorphosis and maturity as writer and thinker; and...an insight into the author's views on the role of the black writer in America." The study aims to show Williams' concern with the Black writer's understanding and depicting of history and that the craft of fiction is as important as content.

Fenderson, Lewis H. "The New Breed of Black Writers and Their Jaundiced View of Tradition." *CLA Journal,* 15 (September 1971), 18-24.

Williams' *Sons of Darkness, Sons of Light* has a protagonist whose "reaction is overt and projected." As one of the new Black writers, he looks askance at tradition.

Fleming, Roger E. "The Nightmare Level of *The Man Who Cried I Am.*" *Contemporary Literature,* 14 (Spring 1973), 186-196.

Williams' "use of bizarre and horrible metaphors for racial conflict and the plight of the black American" has allowed him to escape the natualistic protest novel tradition. He shows the psychological problems of the Black American and the social conditions which foster these problems. The nightmare elements of the novel include sexual perversions, cannibalism and the protagonist's impending death from rectal cancer.

—. " 'Playing the Dozens' in the Black Novel." *Studies in Black Literature,* 3 (Autumn 1972), 23-24.

The dozens is employed by Black writers for many reasons. Williams employs it in *The Man Who Cried I Am* to reinforce the theme of the novel. Max Reddick, in spite of all of his accomplishments, is Black and still an outsider.

Gayle, Addison, Jr. *The Way of the New World: The Black Novel in America.* Garden City, New York: Anchor Press/Doubleday, 1975, pp. 277-286.

Williams' "novels...evidence a steady progression from protest to assertion, from feeble optimism to a hard-learned reality." His strength is in "the synthesis of fiction and history," not "unrelieved protest."

—. "Williams, John A(lfred)." *Contemporary Novelists.* Edited by James Vinson. New York: St. Martin's, 1972, pp. 1355-1356.

Biographical data, list of publications, comments by Williams and a discussion of his novels: *The Angry Ones, Night Song, Sissie, The Man Who Cried I Am* and *Sons of Darkness, Sons of Light.*

Henderson, David. *"The Man Who Cried I Am:* A Critique." *Black Expressions: Essays by and About Black Americans in the Creative Arts.* Edited by Addison Gayle, Jr. New York: Weybright and Talley, 1969, pp. 365-371.

Black people, even though they have not shared in the mainstream of American life, have not remained free of its materialism and competitiveness. When Blacks make their drive for a share of the spoils, the government counteracts with a plan such as the King Alfred Plan—the extermination of American Blacks.

Jackson, Blyden. "The Ghetto of the Negro Novel: A Theme With Variations." *The Discovery of English, NCTE Distinguished Lectures.* Urbana, Illinois: National Council of Teachers of English, 1971, pp. 2-12.

The Negro novel over the last seventy years may well have represented four variations on a theme—the ghetto. Williams' *The Man Who Cried I Am* is representative of the fourth variation: guard the ghetto, it is not to be abandoned.

"John A. Williams: The Black Writer Who Cried I Am." *The Dark and Feeling: Black American Writers and Their Works.* Clarence Major. New York: The Third Press, 1974, pp. 85-94.

Major chronicles Williams' writing career, his ideas about art and his admiration for Chester Himes and Richard Wright. Some biographical data is included.

"John A. Williams." *Dark Symphony: Negro Literature in America.* Edited by James A. Emanuel and Theodore L. Gross. New York: Free Press, 1968, pp. 392-393.

Biographical and critical statement and a brief discusssion of "Son in the Afternoon."

"John A. Williams." *Interviews with Black Writers.* Edited by John O'Brien. New York: Liveright, 1973, pp. 225-243.

His themes are racial, social and political for he believes Black writers are forced to face these issues. He sees man as having to struggle with guilt, his and his race's past. The ultimate solution to the problem is love; and, as a realistic writer, he tries to show this. The novel is changing from a "straight ahead" form to one of improvisation. He discusses his novels and influences.

This interview also appears in *The American Scholar,* Summer 1973.

Klotman, Phyllis R. "An Examination of the Black Confidence Man in two Black Novels: *The Man Who Cried I Am* and *dem.*" *American Literature,* 44 (January 1973), 596-611.

Williams' *The Man Who Cried I Am* develops con men who dupe or con their own. Two Black expatriate authors who have a plan of the United States Government's for genocide are eliminated by two Black espionage agents.

Lewald, H. Ernest, editor. *The Cry of Home: Cultural Nationalism and the Modern Writer.* Knoxville: The University of Tennessee Press, 1972, pp. 230-235.

Williams is one of the new Black writers who has gone beyond anger and become "involved in the larger world of art and ideology."

Peavy, Charles D. "Four Black Revolutionary Novels, 1899-1970." *Journal of Black Studies,* 1 (December 1970), 219-223.

Williams' *Sons of Darkness, Sons of Light* describes organized mass violence, resulting from the sickness of the American society. It is written as a warning to whites, and says that the final response to the Negro question is annihilation—confrontation is unavoidable.

Schraufnagel, Noel. *From Apology to Protest: The Black American Novel.* Deland, Florida: Everett/Edwards, Inc., 1973, pp. 148-151, 187-192.

Williams in his first three novels establishes for the sixties the apologetic novel; "he also presents the theme of interracial sexual relationships." However, by the late sixties, he had turned to militant fiction.

"Seeking a Humanist Level: Interview with John A. Williams." *Arts in Society,* 10 (Spring-Summer 1973), 94-99.

He discusses Black writers, American government, Attica and radical groups with John O'Brien, the interviewer.

Smith, Anneliese H. "A Pain in the Ass: Metaphor in John A. Williams' *The Man Who Cried I Am.*" *Studies in Black Literature,* 3 (Autumn 1972), 25-27.

Reddick's rectal concern is a barometer of his experience, growth and his denial "of the opportunity to live fully."

Starke, Catherine Juanita. *Black Portraiture in American Fiction: Stock Characters, Archetypes and Individuals.* New York: Basic Books, Inc., 1971, pp. 231-236, 239-240.

Williams' Max Reddick in *The Man Who Cried I Am* is a cross between the token Black and the Black Avenger. The latter character type is also used in *Sons of Darkness, Sons of Light.*

"Two Celebrated Authors Say Blacks Facing Genocide in the United States." *Jet,* 41 (October 14, 1971), 46-47.

This is the report of a Black Journal debate. It details how Williams got the idea for *The Man Who Cried I Am,* and he along with Samuel Yette show the relevancy and timelessness of their works.

Walcott, Ronald. "The Early Fiction of John A. Williams." *CLA Journal,* 16 (December 1972), 198-213.

Williams, a serious and prolific writer, in his early fiction included both the pastoral and the political and ended on an optimistic note. However, his third novel, *Sissie,* finds him accepting his experiences which said the America of which he dreamed did not exist. There is still an affirmation, but it is in the acceptance of truth and the refusal to lie. There is developed within these novels, the search motif which also appears in his *This is My Country Too, a Holiday* magazine assignment in which he chronicles his journey through America.

—. "*The Man Who Cried I Am:* Crying in the Dark." *Studies in Black Literature,* 3 (Spring 1972), 24-32.

Williams has always been concerned with the political, but his
novels become more and more violent—there has always been a
certain preoccupation with the subject. His novels can be divided
into two phases—the "first three...attempt to explore those possibilities which lie 'beyond anger' while the last two [*Sons of Darkness, Sons of Light* and *The Man Who Cried I Am*] seek to offer a
stratagem for survival." The first "three can be seen as a search
for the light, the last two are a cry in the dark."

Walton, Martha R. Ballard. "Major Concerns of the Black
Novel in America in Relation to the American Mainstream." Ph.D. dissertation, University of Denver, 1973.

John A. Williams' *The Man Who Cried I Am* has a "picaresque
quality" which allows him " 'to deal with the dilemmas of the
Black Writer, of interracial marriages, and of Black genocide.' "

"Williams, John Alfred." *Black American Writers Past and
Present: A Biographical and Bibliographical Dictionary.*
Theressa Gunnels Rush, Carol Fairbanks Myers and
Esther Spring Arata. Metuchen, New Jersey: The Scare-
crow Press, Inc., 1975. II, 773-776.

Listed are all known published works, criticism of Williams and
biographical data.

Williams, John A. *Flashbacks: A Twenty-Five Year Diary
of Article Writing.* Garden City, New York: Anchor
Press/Doubleday, 1973.

Williams says these articles are "about being a black writer in the
U.S." They span a period from the early 1950's to 1971.

"Williams, John A." *Living Black American Authors: A Biographical Directory.* Ann Allen Shockley and Sue P.
Chandler. New York: Bowker, 1973, pp. 172-173.

Biographical data: birth, education, family, professional experience, publications and address.

D. *The Man Who Cried I Am*

Fleming, Thomas J. "Empty Victory." *The New York Times Book Review,* 29 October 1967, p. 66.

The writer's main character traverses the U.S.A., Europe and Africa, but "never really leaves [escapes] Harlem." The author "cries, with humor and anger, pride and passion, I am."

Joyce, Barbara. "Satire and Alienation in Soulsville." *Phylon,* 29 (Winter 1968), 411-412.

This is a novel which is encyclopedic in tendencies and covers happenings between World War II and 1964. Williams keeps "a good grip on two main characters and many minor ones."

Kersh, Gerald. "Black Man and White Devils." *Saturday Review,* 28 October 1967, pp. 34-35, 40.

"John A. Williams...a first-rate talent of unquestionable authenticity, and the peer of any man writing today" has given "as delicate and perceptive a study of the loneliness of the writer by compulsion as has ever been written."

Simon, Alvin. "A Literary Masterpiece." *Freedomways,* 8 (1968), 79-80.

In this book, John A. Williams shows himself to be so skilled in writing that "it becomes difficult to tell where fiction ends and facts begin." The book "illuminates the duplicity of white America in all its murky recesses."

Sons of Darkness, Sons of Light

"Eye for an Eye." *Time,* 11 July 1969, p. 80.

The story of "the grievances of a man rather than a people," in which Williams attacks "hypocritical blacks as...[well as] complacent whites" and expresses the idea of "role fatigue."

Fleming, Thomas J. Review of *Sons of Darkness, Sons of Light* by John A. Williams. *The New York Times Book Review*, 29 January 1969, p. 4.

This is an open-ended thriller with a "bitter-sweet trace of hope... intertwined with...anger" and a tone which is "somber—and at times, savagely cynical."

Long, Robert Emmet. Review of *Sons of Darkness, Sons of Light* by John A. Williams. *Saturday Review*, 4 October 1969, p. 48.

This is a "sensational novel that exploits violence and fear instead of exploring the contemporary issues underlying them."

Captain Blackman

Cash, Earl A. Review of *Captain Blackman* by John A. Williams. *Black World*, 22 (June 1973), 51-52, 86-88.

An interview in which Cash and Williams discuss this historical novel: his purpose, some of the names—Woodcock, Mimosa, Abraham Blackman; techniques. Included in this review is a response to the book by Williams' son.

—. Review of *Captain Blackman* by John A. Williams. *Negro History Bulletin*, 35 (November 1972), 167.

Williams has remained true to "his imaginative story as well as to the actual events of the past" in this historical novel.

Davis, George. Review of *Captain Blackman* by John A. Williams. *The New York Times Book Review*, 21 May 1972, pp. 4, 14.

This is Williams' most ambitious work; "the past and the present are laid out together." However, it is to be regretted that he was not as innovative in his use of language as in his structure.

Kent, George E. "Outstanding Works in Black Literature During 1972." *Phylon*, 34 (December 1973), 307-329.

Williams explores the fate of Black men in the military history of America. In this book he covers "a considerable amount of history," is not obscure, is inventive. The novel is "very successful in dramatizing brutal suppression," but there is little development of Blackman as a character; he seems to have "little need to search or discover." The book represents a new shape for the historical novel.

Sale, Roger. "Plunging into Life." *The New York Review of Books*, 5 October 1972, pp. 34-36.

"Williams' fictional device is clumsy, and many of his attempts to flesh out history are vulgar, [but] the central vision is one worth reading."

Walker, Jim. Review of *Captain Blackman* by John A. Williams. *Black Creation*, 4 (Fall 1972), 58-59.

Williams has woven into this historical novel a variety of fictional elements in order to merge reality and dream. The lessons/truths of the novel are many and they have the ring of truth.

Mothersill and the Foxes

Foote, Bud. "Williams." *The National Observer*, 29 March 1975, p. 21.

This has the same objectivity and main push, "the hero wants nothing more than communion," as his other books.

Morgan, Marcyliena. Review of *Mothersill and the Foxes* by John A. Williams. *Black Books Bulletin*, 3 (Fall 1975), pp. 35-36.

"That Mothersill is a Black man is coincidental. He possesses no real understanding of Black culture." Therefore, this is a "sad tale of a sorry man and women who sour to his touch."

Perkins, Heul D. Review of *Mothersill and the Foxes* by John A. Williams. *Black World,* 24 (June 1975), 89-91.

This book reinforces the sexual prowess myth of the Black man. The novel is entertaining, not profound and has a surprise ending. "Odell Mothersill is indeed a 'mother' of a man."

CHARLES STEVENSON WRIGHT (1932—)

A. Charles Wright was born in New Franklin, Missouri, on June 4, 1932. He attended public school in Missouri and Lowney Handy Writers Colony in Marshall, Illinois. He began his writing career as a teenager with a regular column in the *Kansas City Call.*

B. Wright, Charles. *The Wig: A Mirror Image.* New York: Farrar, 1966.

Lester Jefferson, a Harlem Negro, decides he will get a share of the "Great Society" promised all Americans. Using Silky Smooth Hair Relaxer, he straightens and yellows his hair. He assumes his "wig" will be his badge of entry. He and his friend, Little Jimmie, try to make it in the recording business, but he has no skill. He tries to work his way up the ladder to attain the American Dream. He assumes several roles in an attempt to be what he thinks others want him to be.

C. Campenni, Frank. "Wright, Charles (Stevenson)." *Con-*

temporary Novelists. Edited by James Vinson. New York: St. Martin's, 1972, pp. 1405-1407.

Biographical data, list of his publications, statements by Wright and a discussion of *The Messenger* and *The Wig* are given.

"Charles Wright." *Interviews with Black Writers.* Edited by John O'Brien. New York: Liveright, 1973, pp. 245-257.

He erases the line between the real and the fantastic—the real world is the best source for fantasy—by avoiding a linear development. The main character in *The Messenger* (fantasy) and *The Wig* (realism) try to fit into the "great society" and do all they can to fit. He was influenced by Hemingway and Katherine Anne Porter.

Foster, Frances S. "Charles Wright: Black Black Humorist." *CLA Journal,* 15 (September 1971), 44-53.

Wright is a minority within a minority. The chief reason for labeling him a Black Humorist is his pre-occupation with reality and illusion and his failure to pass judgment. The form and content of *The Wig* give us a picture of his suggested reality.

Klinkowitz, Jerome. "The New Black Writer and the Old Black Art: Jerome Klinkowitz on Charles Wright." *Fiction International,* 1 (Fall 1973), 123-127.

Wright's three works present the "usual 'search for meaning' theme in a radical new form: imaginative literature, and ultimately fantasy." He, like Nathanael Hawthorne and Franz Kafka, goes past the reality of our lives toward what is actually going on.

Sedlack, Robert P. "Jousting with Rats: Charles Wright's *The Wig.*" *Satire Newsletter,* 7 (Fall 1969), 37-39.

Wright satirizes the abortive efforts of Lester Jefferson, the picaresque hero of *The Wig,* to succeed via white standards and he emphasizes this in Chaper 12. In this chaper, he employs many of the traditional conventions of the mock heroic—"invocation, description of the combatants, speeches including challenges, defiances, boasts, and an elaborate battle scene."

Schraufnagel, Noel. *From Apology to Protest: The Black American Novel.* Deland, Florida: Everett/Edwards, Inc., 1973, pp. 122-123.

Charles Wright's *The Messenger* develops the existential theme of man as an outsider.

Schulz, Max F. *Black Humor Fiction of the Sixties: A Pluralistic Definition of Man and His World.* Athens, Ohio: Ohio University Press, 1973, pp. 9, 99-101, 108-114, 119-122, 151.

The Wig shows man's anxieties growing out of a lack of history or place, a "disenfranchisement from the human race," man's nonentity and the individual's inability to control his own future no matter how much he conforms. "The major tensions of the language of the novel reside in the ambivalent anti-thesis between the white view of the American Negro and the Black-American view of Whitey." The uncertainty of the times is underscored by the shifting point of view and the tone and language switch from the literal to the ironic.

Wright, Charles. *Absolutely Nothing to Get Alarmed About.* New York: Farrar, 1973.

Wright tells the story of his life in a mixture of fact and fiction.

"Wright, Charles Stevenson." *Black American Writers Past and Present: A Biographical and Bibliographical Dictionary.* Theressa Gunnels Rush, Carol Fairbanks Myers and Esther Spring Arata. Metuchen, New Jersey: The Scarecrow Press, Inc., 1975. II, 783-785.

Biographical data, photograph and works by and about him are given.

"Wright, Charles Stevenson." *Contemporary Authors.* Edited

by Clare D. Kinsmon and Mary Ann Tennenhous. Detroit, Michigan: Gale Reserach Company, 1974. IX-XII, 979.

Biographical data: personal, career, writings, works in progress, sidelights, avocational interests and biographical/critical sources.

D. *The Wig*

Fuller, Hoyt W. Review of *The Wig* by Charles S. Wright. *Negro Digest,* 15 (August 1966), 81-82.

The Wig abounds in irony and humor—bitter and black—but has shortcomings.

Hairston, Loyle. "De Sade Up-Dated." *Freedomways,* 6 (1966), 274-275.

The novel represents the tragedy of a Black writer. Wright has fallen victim to the general epidemic of writing of only sex, horror and insanity.

"Other New Fiction." *The Times Literary Supplement,* 9 March 1967, p. 199.

The comic and the horrific never drift too far apart in this "sickeningly true" and unrelenting satire by Charles Wright.

Smith, William James. Review of *The Wig* by Charles Wright. *Commonweal,* 29 April 1966, pp. 182-183.

The novel is short, episodic, bizarre, but is not successful as a whole because Wright places his faith in black humor to "sustain attention."

Teachout, Peter R. "East-West Sons of Huck Finn." *The Nation,* 18 April 1966, pp. 466-467.

On the surface, the book is awkward; however, on another level

it is an incorporation of the Faustian legend, *Candide,* and shack-
led Jim in *The Adventures of Huckleberry Finn.*

SARAH E. WRIGHT

A. Sarah E. Wright was born in Wetipquin, Maryland. She attended Howard University, the University of Pennsylvania,
Cheyney State Teachers College and New School for Social
Work. She has worked as teacher, bookkeeper and office
manager.

B. Wright, Sarah E. *This Child's Gonna Live.* New York:
Delacorte Press, 1969.

Mariah Upsur, a resident of Tangierneck in Maryland, is the wife of
Jacob, a dreamer, and the mother of three children—Skeeter,
Rabbit and Gezee. It centers on her children—born, dead and
about-to-be-born—her husband and her desire to escape the land
of death to which they seem chained.

C. Land, Irene Stokvis, editor. "First Novelists." *Library Journal,* 94 (February 1, 1969), 582.

Wright gives brief biographical data and her views on her writing.

Schraufnagel, Noel. *From Apology to Protest: The Black
American Novel.* Deland, Florida: Everett/Edwards,
Inc., 1973, pp. 170-171.

Wright's *This Child's Gonna Live* presents a deep picture of violence, examines the sexual aspects of racism and is "a study of the

psychological effects of white oppression."

Whitlow, Roger. *Black American Literature: A Critical History.* Chicago: Nelson Hall, 1973, pp. 162-165.

Brief biographical data and a discussion *This Child's Gonna Live.*

"Wright, Sarah E." *Black Writers Past and Present: A Biographical and Bibliographical Dictionary.* Theressa Gunnells Rush, Carol Fairbanks Myers and Esther Spring Arata. Metuchen, New Jersey: The Scarecrow Press, Inc., 1975.

Biographical data, criticism by and about the author, comments by her and her known published works are given.

"Wright, Sarah E." *Contemporary Authors.* Edited by Clare D. Kisman and Mary Ann Tennenhouse. Detroit, Michigan: Gale Research Company, 1973. XXVII-XL, 574.

Biographical data: personal, career, writings, work in progress and biographical/critical sources.

D. *This Child's Gonna Live*

"American Nightmare." *The Times Literary Supplement,* 16 October 1969, p. 1177.

There is something spurious and sentimental about the novel even though "the harshness is probably not exaggerated."

Amini, Johari (Jewel C. Latimore). Review of *This Child's Gonna Live* by Sarah E. Wright. *Negro Digest,* 18 (August 1969), 51-52.

This novel/poem is full of veracity about Black marriage and the Black family.

Clarke, John Henrik. "Capturing Black Family Survival."

Freedomways, 10 (1970), 278-279.

This is a folk novel which celebrates life.

Stevens, Shane. Review of *This Child's Gonna Live* by Sarah
E. Wright. *The New York Times Book Review,* 29 January 1969, pp. 4-5.

This book is an "impressive achievement as "a celebration of life over death."

FRANK GARVIN YERBY (1916—)

A. Frank Garvin Yerby was born in Augusta, Georgia, on September 5, 1916. He attended Paine College, Fisk University and the University of Chicago. He has been a teacher and laboratory technician and is now a full time writer. In 1944, he won the O'Henry Memorial Award for his short story "Health Card." Yerby is the most prolific and commercially successful Black American writer to date.

B. Yerby, Frank. *An Odor of Sanctity: A Novel of Medieval Moorish Spain.* New York: Dial, 1965.

Alaris, a tenth-century Gothic Spanish nobleman, ends up being a Christian saint martyred by the Moors. This comes after a very unorthodox and unChristian life.

—. *Goat Song: A Novel of Ancient Greece.* New York: Dial, 1968.

Ariston, an indescribably beautiful fifth century B. C. Spartan, is

189

caught trying to steal a young goat. His plight is magnified when he is accused falsely of incest, decides heterosexual love is better, and has a number of adventures on land and sea. He is captured and taken to Athens as slave and prostitute. At the same time, he tries to win Athenian citizenship for himself.

—. *Judas, My Brother: the Story of the Thirteenth Disciple.* New York: Dial, 1968.

This is the story of Nathan bar Yehudah and Yeshu'a ha Notzri. Nathan bar Yehudah is a wealthy, skeptic, hedonist with a love for the flesh who marries Yeshu'a's younger sister. Yeshu'a ha Notzri, Jesus of Nazareth, is plagued by his belief that he is illegitimate. He, however, accomplishes "miracles" and provokes the Romans and Hebrews by establishing an ascetic and fanatical sect and finally dies at their hands.

—. *Speak Now: A Modern Novel.* New York: Dial, 1969.

A Negro jazz musician in Paris meets the white heiress of a tobacco company who is alone and pregnant. They agree to marry so the child will have a name, then divorce and no one will know she married a Negro. However, they fall in love.

—. *The Dahomean: An Historical Novel.* New York: Dial, 1971.

This is the story of Nyasanu, son of an African chieftain, who has been stolen and sold at a slave auction in Virginia. His life story from boyhood and youthful romance through war, grief, love and a leader of men is chronicled.

—. *The Girl from Storyville: A Victorian Novel.* New York: Dial, 1972.

Fanny Turner, reared lovelessly by her father and stepmother in Shreveport and New Orleans, tries to kill her stepmother before she is eight. Later, she is gang raped, impregnated and joins a brothel from which she is rescued. The man who rescues her also marries her, but she is dissatisfied and seeks a man as repulsive as she thinks herself.

—. *The Voyage Unplanned.* New York: Dial, 1974.

John Farrow, a former O.S.S. officer, is searching for a young French Lady of the Resistance he rescued from the Nazis twenty-eight years before the book opens. He meets and falls in love with an Israeli agent who is the sister and an exact replica of his lost love. The problem is whether he is in love with her or a memory and whether she is using him to entrap a former Nazi.

—. *Tobias and the Angel.* New York: Dial, 1975.

Tobias Tobit's friend Angie, an angel, shepherds him through various amorous adventures. Tobias finally falls into the clutches of twin sisters and marries one of them; it is uncertain which.

C. Campenni, Frank. "Yerby, Frank (Garvin)." *Contemporary Novelists.* Edited by James Vinson. New York: St. Martin's, 1972, pp. 1416-1419.

Biographical data, list of publications, Yerby's comments about his intent and Campenni's discussion of Yerby's works.

Graham, Maryemma. "Frank Yerby, King of the Costume Novel." *Essence,* 6 (October 1975), 70-71, 88-89, 91-92.

Frank Yerby after years of creating "the most popular love-lust-war fiction" is beginning to erase "some of the corn." In spite of his castigation of the South in his early pot-boilers, he believes "the hope of the Black man is in the South."

Hill, James Lee. "Bibliography of the Works of Chester Himes, Ann Petry and Frank Yerby." *Black Books Bulletin,* 3 (Fall 1975), 60-72.

Yerby's works and biographical and critical works about him are listed. Some of the secondary sources are annotated.

Frank Garvin Yerby

Hill, William Werdna, Jr. "Behind the Magnolia Mask: Frank Yerby as Critic of the South." M. A. thesis, Auburn University, 1968.

Most critics assert that Frank Yerby is a writer of "raceless" fiction. However, a study of his early short stories and nine of his novels show him to be a writer of racial and regional protest.

Schraufnagel, Noel. *From Apology to Protest: The Black American Novel.* Deland, Florida: Everett/Edwards, Inc., 1973, pp. 155-157.

Yerby's *Speak Now* is another "version of the black expatriate and his struggle to escape or to come to terms with racism."

Turner, Darwin T. "Frank Yerby as Debunker." *Massachusetts Review,* 9 (Summer 1968), 569-577.

Yerby has weaknesses as a craftsman, but his soap opera fiction is "anti-romantic, existentialist melodrama which is frequently as satirical as Voltaire's *Candide*." He debunks historical myths and has attacked America—North and South—Negroes, white males and females, war, colonists, reconstruction, crusaders and myths of other lands. He has, however, a positive philosophy—he believes "men succeed and are extolled because they are smarter, stronger, bolder and braver than others."

This article is reprinted in *The Black Novelist* edited by Robert Hemenway.

—. "Frank Yerby: Golden Debunker." *Black Books Bulletin,* 1 (Spring/Summer 1972), 5-9, 30-33.

Yerby's novelistic formula and theory are discussed and illustrated. Yerby debunks myths which exist, including the one man one woman romantic one on which his formulaic novels are predicated.

"Yerby, Frank." *Black American Writers Past and Present: A Biographical and Bibliographical Dictionary.* Theressa Gunnels Rush, Carol Fairbanks Myers and Esther Spring

192

Arata. Metuchen, New Jersey: The Scarecrow Press, Inc., 1975. II, 793-795.

Listed are his known published works and some sources of biographical data and criticism.

"Yerby, Frank G(arvin)." *Contemporary Authors.* Edited by Clare D. Kinsman and Mary Ann Tennenhouse. Detroit, Michigan: Gale Research Company, 1974. IX-XII, 985-986.

Biographical data: personal, career, writings, sidelights, avocational interests and biographical/critical sources.

D. *An Odor of Sanctity*

Review of *An Odour of Sanctity* by Frank Yerby. *Times Literary Supplement,* 28 July 1966, p. 656.

"The story itself has much inherent interest, but Mr. Yerby's panoramic ambitions render it rather formless."

Judas, My Brother

Turner, Darwin T. Review of *Judas, My Brother* by Frank Yerby. *Negro Digest,* 18 (April 1969), 80-82.

Yerby's twenty-second novel is an interpretation of "the greatest story ever told" which he documents. He diverges from the Gospels and scholarly tradition. He attacks the Pauline myth, thus stimulating the reader to question and seek an answer.

Speak Now

Turner, Darwin T. Review of *Speak Now* by Frank Yerby. *Negro Digest,* 19 (February 1970), 79-81.

This is "Yerby's first novel about a Negro protagonist." Here, there are "caustic denunciations of white racism," but his format—

Al Young

"the protagonist is an outcast...three...heroines (the perfect wife, the woman of established society, and the sex goddess)...warfare... the sex goddess is raped; the myths of history are debunked"— remains the same though the skin color of the protagonist has changed.

The Dahomean

Turner, Darwin T.   Review of *The Dahomean* by Frank Yerby.   *Black World,* 21 (February 1972), 51-52, 84-87.

This book is superior to Yerby's earlier best sellers; it "supports [his] ...philosophy that worldly success is determined...by strength, intelligence and ruthlessness..."   In this costume novel, he has woven fiction and history to show nineteenth century Africa. Those things which have previously been considered weaknesses become strengths—using foreign terms in dialogue for authenticity, digressions into essays to give historical data and an over reliance on chance.   He presents an exciting and illuminating history of Black people—all are not virtuous—and a focus on a Black hero.

AL YOUNG (1939—)

A. Al Young was born in Ocean Springs, Mississippi, on May 31, 1939.   He attended the University of Michigan, Stanford University and the University of California, Berkeley.   He has been a free-lance musician, disk jockey, instructor, consultant and writer.   He won the Wallace E. Stegner Fellowship in Creative Writing, the Joseph Henry Jackson Award of the San Francisco Foundation for dancing and the National Endowment for the Arts Grant for Poetry.   For several years as Jones Lecturer, he conducted writing and literature classes at Stanford.

B. Young, Al. *Snakes.* New York: Holt, 1970.

> This is the story of MC, a Black youth interested in music. Or-
> phaned at an early age, he lives with his grandmother, Claude. He
> and his drummer friend, Shakes, form a band along with Champ
> another friend. They play the school gigs, parties, TV talent show
> and cut the record "Snakes" which becomes a local hit. MC finally
> leaves home for New York.

—. *Who is Angelina?* New York: Holt, 1975.

> Angelina Green—a young, educated Black woman—searches for
> her identity and purpose in life. Her odyssey toward self-discovery
> takes her from California to Mexico to Detroit.

C. "Al Young." *Interviews with Black Writers.* Edited by John
O'Brien. New York: Liveright, 1973, pp. 259-269.

> The dance, which is the natural movement of life, is the controlling
> image in his poetry and fiction. He feels the cyclical theory of
> history and evolution is operative, and man must unite with others
> to find the dance in life. He is influenced by music. He discusses
> his poetry and his fiction.

> This interview appears in the *New Orleans Review* for Summer
> 1973.

Land, Irene Stokvis, editor. "First Novelists." *Library Journal,* 95 (February 1, 1970), 525.

> Young discusses his novel, *Snakes.*

"Young, Al." *Black American Writers Past and Present: A
Biographical and Bibliographical Dictionary.* Theressa
Gunnels Rush, Carol Fairbanks Myers, and Esther Spring
Arata. Metuchen, New Jersey: The Scarecrow Press,
Inc., 1975. II, 795-797.

> Biographical data, photograph, a list of his known works and a

statement by Young.

"Young, Al." *Contemporary Authors.* Edited by Clare D. Kinsman and Mary Ann Tennenhouse. Detroit, Michigan: Gale Research Company, 1972. XXIX-XXXII, 701.

Biographical data: personal, career, writings, work in progress, sidelights and biographical/critical sources.

C. Young, Al. "Statement on Aesthetics, Poetics, Kinetics." *New Black Voices: An Anthology of Contemporary Afro-American Literature.* Edited by Abraham Chapman. New York: Mentor Books, 1972, pp. 553-554.

Writing—poetry or the novel—is a way "of reaching out...of seeing, a way of saying: 'I live in the world too and this is my way of being here with you.' "

D. *Who is Angelina?*

Palm, Roberta. Review of *Who is Angelina?* by Al Young. *Black World,* 24 (September 1975), 88-89.

"Young is as alienated from his character as she is described to be from herself and her peers." However, "his characters speak with realistic tone and in genuine cadence" which provides a bright spot.

SOURCES CONSULTED

Alexander, Jean A. "Black Literature for the 'Culturally Deprived' Curriculum: Who Are the Losers?" *Negro American
Literature Forum*, 4 (Fall 1970), 96-103.

Baker, Augusta. *The Black Experience in Children's Books.*
New York: New York Public Library, 1971.

Black World. A Monthly publication devoted to critical and creative writing by Blacks, as well as monthly reports on current
events relating to Blacks. Now defunct.

CLA Journal. Official quarterly publication of the College
Language Associaion, consisting primarily of teachers of
English and modern language in Black colleges.

Corrigan, Robert A. "Afro-American Fiction: A Checklist
1853-1970." *Midcontinent American Studies Journal*, 11
(Summer 1971), 114-135.

Curl, Charles H. "Black Studies: Form and Content." *CLA
Journal*, 13 (September 1969), 1-9.

Deodene, Frank and William P. French. *Black American Fiction
Since 1952: A Preliminary Checklist.* Chatham, New Jersey:
The Chatham Bookseller, 1970.

Dodds, Barbara. *Negro Literature for High School Students.*
Champaign, Illinois: National Council of Teachers of English, 1968.

Farrison, W. Edward. "What American Negro Literature Exists

and Who Should Teach it?" *CLA Journal,* 13 (June 1970), 374-381.

Ford, Nick Aaron. "Black Literature and the Problem of Evaluation." *College English,* 32 (February 1971), 536-547.

—. *Black Studies: Threat or Challenge.* Port Washington, New York: Kennikat Press, 1973.

—. "What Every English Teacher Should Know About Black Studies." *The CEA Critic,* 36 (May 1974), 19-27.

—, Donald B. Gibson and Charles A. Ray. "Black Literature: Problems and Opportunities—A Sympsium." *CLA Journal,* 13 (September 1969), 10-20.

Freedomways. A quarterly review.

Hach, Clarence W. "Introduction to Syllabus on Afro-American Literature." *Illinois English Bulletin,* 58 (November 1970), 2-4.

Jeffers, Lance. "Afro-American Literature, The Conscience of Man." *The Black Scholar,* 2 (January 1971), 47-53.

Johnson, Harry Alleyn, editor. *Multimedia Materials for Afro-American Studies: A Curriculum Orientation and Annotated Bibliography of Resources.* New York: Bowker, 1971.

Klotman, Phyllis. "An Approach to the Teaching of Black Literature—Or: What's a White Lady Like You Doing in a Class Like This?" *The CEA Critic,* 34 (January 1972), 12-15.

Long, Richard A. "The Black Studies Boondogle." *Liberator,* 10 (September 1970), 6-9.

—. "Black Studies: International Dimensions." *CLA Journal,* 14 (September 1970), 1-6.

McDowell, Robert E. and George Fortenberry. "A Checklist of

Books and Essays About American Negro Novelists." *Studies in the Novel,* 3 (Summer 1971), 219-236.

McPherson, James M., Laurence B. Holland, et al. *Blacks in America: Bibliographical Essays.* New York: Doubleday, 1971.

Phylon. Quarterly review of race and culture.

Reid, Inez Smith, editor. *The Black Prism: Perspectives on the Black Experience.* Brooklyn, New York: Faculty Press, 1969.

Rollins, Charlemae, editor. *We Build Together: A Reader's Guide to Negro Literature for Elementary and High School Use.* Champaign, Illinois: National Council of Teachers of English, 1967.

Rowell, Charles Henry. "Afro-American Literary Bibliographies: An Annotated List of Bibliographical Guides for the Study of Afro-American Literature, Folklore and Related Areas." Ph.D. dissertation, Ohio State University, 1972.

Standley, Fred L. "The Use and Effects of Afro-American Literature." *The CEA Forum,* 4 (April 1974), 2-3.

Sterling, Dorothy. "The Soul of Learning." *The English Journal,* 59 (February 1968), 166-180.

—. 'What's Black and White and Read All Over?" *The English Journal,* 58 (September 1969), 817-832.

Szwed, John F., editor. *Black America.* New York: Basic Books, Inc., 1970.

Turner, Darwin T. *Afro-American Writers.* New York: Appleton, 1970.

— and Barbara Dodds Stanford. *Theory and Practice in the Teaching of Literature by Afro-Americans.* Urbana, Illinois:

Sources Consulted

The National Council of Teachers of English/The Educational Resources Information Center, 1971.

Whitlow, Roger. *Black American Literature: A Critical History.* Chicago: Nelson Hall, 1973.

Whiteman, Maxwell. *A Century of Fiction by American Negroes 1853-1952: A Descriptive Bibliography.* N.P.: Albert Saifer, 1974.

Williams, Ora. *American Black Women in the Arts and Social Sciences: A Bibliographic Survey.* Metuchen, New Jersey: The Scarecrow Press, Inc., 1973.

INDEX OF TITLES:
NOVELS AND SHORT STORY COLLECTIONS

201

Index of Titles

Index of Titles

Youngblood by John O. Killens, 110, 111

Z

Zeely by Virginia Hamilton, 73

INDEX OF AUTHORS

Index of Authors

Byrd, James W., 133

C

Cade, Toni, 146
Cain, George, 38-39
Caldwell, Stephen F., 170
Campenni, Frank J., 79, 183, 191
Canary, Robert H., 51
Carter, Tom, 66
Cash, Earl A., 94, 174, 181
Chapman, Abraham, 168
Chelminski, Rudolph, 80
Childress, Alice, 40-41
Clarke, John Henrik, 126, 188
Coleman, Horace W., Jr., 158
Coles, Robert, 163
Collier, Eugenia, 12, 158
Colter, Cyrus, 42-44
Coombs, Orde, 27
Cooper, Arthur, 142
Cooper, Clarence, Jr., 44-45
Cornish, Sam, 163
Cortez, Rochell, 124
Cosgrove, William, 12

D

Dance, Daryl C(umber), 12, 35, 41, 80, 101
Darden, Norman, 96
Davis, Arthur P., 16, 80, 166
Davis, George, 37, 45-46, 62, 112, 117, 181
Davis, L. J., 63, 153
Davis, Lester, 168
Davis, Nolan, 46-47
Dee, Ruby, 69, 128

Delany, Samuel R., 48-55
Del Rey, Lester, 53, 54
Demby, William, 55-59
Dempsey, David, 32
Donoso, Jose, 133
Duff, Gerald, 142

E

Earles, Horace, 152
Ebert, Roger, 140, 171
Eckman, Fern Marja, 13
Edwards, Thomas R., 24, 135, 148
Elder, Lonne, III, 34
Emanuel, James A., 13, 165
Evans, Don, 35

F

Fabre, Michel, 13, 80, 81
Fair, Ronald L., 59-62
Farnsworth, Robert M., 43
Fenderson, Lewis H., 33, 142, 174
Fisher, Russell G., 13
Flamer, Merrianne, 24
Fleming, Robert E., 61
Fleming, Roger E., 174, 175
Fleming, Thomas J., 180, 181
Foote, Bud, 149, 182
Ford, Nick Aaron, 142
Forrest, Leon, 62-63
Foster, David E., 13
Foster, Frances S., 184
Fowler, Carolyn, 162
Frakes, James R., 112
Frazier, Kermit, 169
Freedman, Richard, 156
Friedman, Alan, 148

Index of Authors

Fuller, Hoyt W., 61, 69, 73, 81, 186

G

Gaines, Ernest J., 64-70
Gayle, Addison, Jr., 14, 39, 67, 81,
  101, 108, 143, 175
George, Felicia, 14, 102
Gérard, Albert, 14
Gibson, Donald B., 14
Giddings, Paula, 165
Gilbert, Zack, 63
Giles, James R., 35, 131, 132
Gilliam, Barry, 54
Gilman, Richard, 22
Giovanni, Nikki, 32, 75, 77, 126
Gordon, Andrew, 148
Gottlieb, Annie, 124
Graham, Maryemma, 191
Grant, Liz, 107, 128, 153
Greenfield, Eloise, 124
Greenlee, Sam, 71-73, 81
Greenya, John, 32
Gross, Barry, 15
Gross, Robert A., 67, 72, 77, 139,
  143, 158
Grosvenor, Dorothy, 47
Gussow, Mel, 159

H

Hairston, Loyle, 63, 138, 151, 171,
  186
Hamilton, Virginia, 73-76
Harper, Howard M., Jr., 16
Hay, Samuel A., 35
Hayashi, Susanna C., 15

Heard, Nathan C., 76-78
Heins, Paul, 75, 76
Henderson, David, 175
Hernton, Calvin C., 15
Hicks, Granville, 157
Hill, James Lee, 82, 191
Hill, William Werdna, Jr., 192
Himes, Chester, 78-86
Hoffman, Nancy Y., 56, 57
Hopkins, Lee Bennett, 75
Hord, Fred, 37
Howe, Irving, 23
Hudson, Jo, 171
Hudson, Theodore R., 136
Hunter, Kristin, 87-89

I

Ihde, Horst, 109
Ivy, Archie, 152

J

Jackson, Blyden, 90-91, 109, 176
Jackson, Jesse, 91-93
Jackson, Kennell, Jr., 36
Jaŕab, Josef, 102
Jefferson, Margo, 96, 129
Johnson, Charles, 93-95
Johnson, Diane, 62
Johnson, Joe, 57
Jonas, Gerald, 54
Jones, Gayl, 95-97
Jones, John Henry, 61, 111
Jordan, June, 98-99
Joyce, Barbara, 146, 180